PAGA

 a beginner's guide

TERESA MOOREY

Headway · Hodder & Stoughton

Dedication

To my mother for giving me the freedom to find my own path.
And to my Mother for showing it to me.

British Library Cataloguing in Publication Data

Vidgen-Moorey, Teresa
Paganism: a beginner's guide
1. Paganism
I. Title
299.1'6

ISBN 0 340 670134

First published 1996
Impression number 10 9 8   7 6   5 4   3 2   1
Year   1999 1998 1997 1996

Illustrations by Dark Moon Designs

Typeset by Transet Limited, Coventry, England
Printed in Great Britain for Hodder & Stoughton Educational, a division of Hodder
Headline plc, 338 Euston Road, London NW1 3BH by Cox and Wyman Limited,
Reading.

CONTENTS

acknowledgements

Special thanks to Shan of the House of the Goddess, for reading over the manuscript, making suggestions for improvements, providing information on pagan contacts and generally being encouraging.

Many thanks to the Pagan Federation for helpful suggestions and to Daniel Cohen of *Wood & Water* magazine for the same.

Thank you to Pete Jennings of the Odinshof Ipswich Hearth and editor of *Gippeswic* magazine for supplying me with the material on the Northern Tradition.

Thanks to Carolyn Finlay of 'Different Drum' for encouragement and suggestions for the Shamanism chapter, and to Leo Rutherford of Eagle's Wing, and Philip Carr – Gomm of OBOD, for helpful information.

Thanks also to the Fellowship of Isis for responding to my request for information, and to the Church of all Worlds and the Pan Pacific Pagan Alliance for Australian information.

Lastly, thanks to all that has empowered me; the writers, mostly listed in these pages that have inspired me; my husband for his support; my children for their tolerance; and the stone of the Cotswolds, the sycamores, herbs, my special stream and meadow of the Otherworld, for the songs they have sung to me.

INTRODUCTION

Paganism is the fastest-growing religion today. Many of us feel we have lost something radical in modern life. Our traditions are impoverished, our dogmas meaningless and our world robbed of its soul. Pagan paths offer ways of rediscovering our mystic heritage and of worshipping without being required to have literal beliefs and lists of rules.

Pagans happily acknowledge their unrestrained love of life and its pleasures, but they also undertake responsibility, for themselves, humanity and the earth. There are many types of pagan spirituality, and only a small minority of pagans actually join any tradition. However, to bring paganism to life we shall be examining some of the options in the following pages. Strictly speaking, what we are talking about is Neo-paganism – something that combines the best of the Old in a way that is relevant to what we are today. The word 'pagan', like 'occult' or 'witch' often evokes knee-jerk reactions. This book seeks to clarify the message of beauty, love and respect that is true paganism.

Please use this book as a starting point to explore further for yourself. Delve into myths and meanings. Think for yourself, for life is an exciting journey; you select your own path in your own way. If pagan ways meet your needs, they can open up whole new stretches of country, but this is your own choice. Take your time to reclaim your personal heritage and your links with the earth, and discover the joy and fulfilment this can yield.

Blessings. Samhain 1995

CHAPTER 1

WHAT IS A PAGAN?

... I'd rather be
A Pagan suckled in a creed outworn;
So might I, standing on this pleasant lea
Have glimpses that would make me less forlorn.

W. Wordsworth, *Sonnets*

PAGAN BELIEFS AND WORSHIP

Pagans love and honour the earth as Mother Goddess, celebrating her cycles and receiving her gifts with joy. They feel a part of all that lives in animals, plants, and the soil itself, and so they treat all with respect. Pagans also find joy in their bodies, for the pleasures of the senses are a gift of the Goddess. They wish to regain a sense of roots and ancestry and to pass on to their children a true feeling of belonging. 'Pagan' is derived from the Latin for 'rustic' or 'peasant'.

Paganism makes no claims to being the only right way. There are no creeds and no single source of 'Truth'. Most pagans do not follow any special tradition, such as Wicca, or Druidry. Sometimes they may join one tradition, then change to another, and then just go off and do their own thing. Freedom is very precious to pagans and they do not seek to control anyone. There are no prophets, although there may be wise people who acquire a following. Prophets are only required when God is separated from the world, and to pagans the world is the Goddess. In a sense each pagan is her/his own prophet.

Pagans are nature-worshippers, finding joy and a sense of true belonging in places of natural beauty. This is probably the single most important common denominator, along with rediscovering old traditions and wisdom, and putting them into practice. Paganism is about true remembering, reclaiming the best in our heritage and leaving behind destruction. Worship may take the form of rituals, complex or simple, or may be largely a matter of attitude. Many people are probably pagans without ever having considered themselves as such. However, we are concerned here with those who designate themselves 'pagan'. Some feel we need to get back to basics and develop a more primitive lifestyle, but many also feel that the way is forward, to a more balanced use of technology. Paganism is often very attractive to city-dwellers who feel they have come adrift from their soil of origin, and as most people live in cities, so most pagans live in cities also – and it is there that most courses in paganism and pagan groups are found.

Who are they?

Pagans are mostly quite ordinary, coming from all walks of life. The popular image of flowing beards, nudity and woodland orgies does not fit the majority of pagans. To be a pagan you do not have to wear special clothes or jewellery, or dance around stone circles. Pagans are found in all types of employment. There are many in the healing professions, for pagans are drawn to healing, and healing the earth – or at least our attitude to Her – is a pagan vocation.

Pagans do not deny room to rage, pain, and violence, for these are part of us and part of nature. However, being conscious of these things does not mean rampant indulgence of them – pagans seek the positive in all aspects, and the one rule that is universal is 'Harm none' which is extremely far-reaching when you think about it. Without winter there is no spring, without rain and grey clouds no blossom. There is anger as well as love, but anger does not destroy love – it can enrich it. Pagans are aware of both sides.

In a sense paganism is a fertility cult and children are treasured and respected. They are brought up to have respect for themselves, for others and for the environment, but they are not forced to believe anything or to participate in anything unless they wish. Pagan parents hope to equip their children to make their own choices, rather than make choices for them. However, pagan families have traditions that focus on the Eight Sabbats, (see Chapter 5), and the idea of living in conscious love of the earth pervades daily life. There is often a household shrine, and artefacts speaking of a pagan faith in the house, and religious ideas are subtly present in many activities.

Worship and ritual

Pagan worship tends to be about action, rather than belief – about what you do, how you feel, the rhythms of your life, how you participate in the world around you. Some pagans like to write rituals, and most take part in rituals, for through them we find ways to unite ourselves with the natural world. Pagan religious observance is closely connected to the cycles of the earth, but doing the garden or going for a walk is a form of worship too.

Religion is about inspirations and quests. To a pagan it is mostly the journey that counts, its many meanings and experiences. In the 'Great Mother Charge' (from a Wiccan ceremony) the Goddess tells us: '... thy seeking and yearning shall avail thee not unless thou knowest the mystery: that if that which thou seekest thou findest not within thee thou wilt never find it without thee: for behold, I have been with thee from the beginning and I am that which is attained at the end of desire.' The message here is quite clear: anything worth finding is inside us. It is a mystical thing, and it cannot be communicated or defined. Hard and fast rules are useless on this type of quest.

4

Above and below

In general the monotheistic, patriarchal religions do not see the body as holy, and by the same token they do not see the world as holy either. Rather, it is there to be exploited; to some even holocaust is acceptable in return for redemption in an afterlife. God is separate from the world and His word is given out by prophets, whose sayings are law. Pagans observe that this is dangerous in more ways than the obvious. It puts power into the hands of people who are not necessarily wise or benevolent and it can even block experience of the divine, for dogma hardly encourages transcendence.

Moreover such an attitude encourages splits – God/Devil, divine/earthly, soul/body, light/dark, man/woman – and such splits often mean that something very valuable ends up cast into shadows and denied. Devil, dark, woman, body, earth have somehow been thrown together and regarded as an evil package. The pagan way is concerned with deep respect for the feminine in all its aspects. That includes the Crone, menstrual blood, sexual seductiveness and 'irrationality', as well the more generally acceptable faces, such as fecund mother and beautiful maiden. Paganism is Goddess worship, and sexual love is Her gift, there to be enjoyed and valued as sacred.

God and gods

We have seen how important the Goddess is, but pagan ideas about divinity are fluid. It is a question of what inspires or feels suitable at a particular place and time. Pagans do not 'believe in' a God or gods. Their religion is one of immanence, which means that divinity is all around us and within us. It is felt and perceived; there is no act of faith. To some, worship of the Great Mother amounts to almost Goddess monotheism. Many worship the Goddess, in her triple aspect, Maiden Mother and Crone and Her consort the Horned God of Nature, but this leaves room for many other deities from ancient pantheons – and also for gods within tree, stone and river. Some pagans always think in terms of Goddess and God, others always in terms of many, and I suspect most think in different ways at different times. Pagans see no inconsistency in this – it's a question of what works for you. We look at ideas of deity later in our chapter 'Goddess and God'.

It seems that life on earth is best perpetuated by many different life forms, feeding off each other and dependent on each other in a variety of ways. Pagans see diversity as essential to the spiritual world also. The idea of one path makes it all too easy to destroy institutions, ideas and people. Polytheism can include monotheism, but the reverse is rarely the case. Paganism is extremely tolerant – for instance there are Christian witches. It never seeks converts, and most pagans do not feel they were 'converted' in any way – they simply returned to what they felt most natural, accepted this, reaffirmed it and extended it. There is no concept of sin, although there may be estrangement – from the earth, nature, or, most importantly, from ourselves. And of course we all have to wear the cloak we weave.

Pagans are united by feeling – a feeling of love, oneness, respect and celebration. Life is more complex than we can understand, and we can extend our reality, our truth, our being by sharing in this. In some ways paganism offers hope for humanity because it trusts us and the essential goodness of us all, regardless of rules and creeds.

PRACTICE

If these ideas are new to you, you may like to give them some deep thought. How do you feel about religion without dogma? What might the benefits be? How has dogma affected your life, the lives of your friends, the nations of the world? What is the point of religion to you? And how do you feel about the earth, nature and the Goddess?

Further information

Adler, Margot, *Drawing Down the Moon*, Beacon, 1986. Definitive survey of paganism, mostly in the United States. Long, but very readable.

Serith, Ceisiwr, *The Pagan Family*, Llewellyn, 1994. Paganism in action in family life with suggestions and rituals – a useful book.

The Pagan Index, an excellent, comprehensive book defining pagan paths and giving a host of contacts and events all over the UK, £5.99 post free, House of the Goddess (see below).

House of the Goddess Information Services and Leaflets: SAE to 33 Oldridge Road, London SW12 8PN. Tel. 0181 673 6370.

Pagan Federation Information Pack, from the Pagan Federation, BM 7097, London WC1N 3XX, England, £2.00 at Samhain 1995. Postage UK 0.75p, Europe £2.25; elsewhere £3.25. For more information send SAE to Pagan Federation.

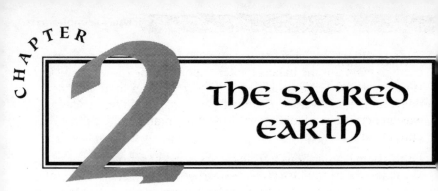

THE SACRED EARTH

Owl guardians dark wings of the night
Laughing otter spills into the stream ...
A mystery unfolding
There's a mystery unfolding
On the land

Carolyn Hillyer, 'A Mystery Unfolding', from the album *Heron Valley* and the book *Two Drumbeats: Songs of the Scared Earth* Seventh Wave Music, 1993

To pagans nature is holy, the earth is holy, and the body is holy. The divine is everywhere, inside us, outside us, around us. Our blood and bones were formed from the minerals of the earth and to them our bodies will eventually return. Womb and tomb, tomb and womb, the spiral unfolds. In this chapter we are concerned mostly with worship, wonderment and participation in the magic that is earth.

The ANCIENTS

Many writers have suggested that the ancients had a very different relationship with the earth from that which we have today. They worshipped her as Goddess, very practically. In *The Ancient British Goddess* Kathy Jones tells us: 'For the long ages of the Paleolithic Era the Goddess reigned alone ... The Earth was Her body ... The people of those times knew about the natural rhythms of Mother

Earth ... They knew how to correctly position stones and mounds in order to maintain the balance and harmony of their Mother's Body.' It seems our ancestors did not build empty shrines to an abstract deity; rather they were sculptors of the sacred, and their worship was an active one of taking part in and maintaining the energy currents of the Earth.

Earth energy can give us a fresh perspective on astrology, as Colin Wilson explains in *Starseekers*. Instead of looking to the stars, and linking their movements with events on earth, we might try to do the reverse. Our foremothers and fathers were very sensitive to the energy patterns in the earth's crust, and only when they noticed fluctuations in these did they make the link with what was happening overhead. So astrology did not arise from people having their heads in the clouds, but from having their feet on the ground and really knowing about the earth they trod. Wilson calls this the 'lunar knowledge' of instinct, as opposed to logical 'solar knowledge'.

Ley Lines

The idea of lines of energy on the earth, or 'ley lines' was first popularised by Alfred Watkins in *The Old Straight Track*. Ley lines appear to run in straight lines that can be drawn on a map, linking sites of ancient importance, such as churches (which were regularly built in pagans' sacred places) and stone circles. In addition they often link places with similar names such as Dorrington and Donnington. Perhaps the best-known English ley runs from St Michael's Mount in Cornwall, through Glastonbury and on, to just north of Lowestoft. Leys are also found in Australia. These are the 'Songlines' of the first Ancestors from the Dreamtime as they travelled over the land, singing the world alive. In America there are many straight line features, notably those left by the extinct Miwok Indians in the California sierras. A little investigation of one's surroundings can often reveal much of interest; for instance, ancient tracks used for many years by native people often follow leys.

Places where several leys intersect are held to be areas of power or disturbance: some prehistoric monuments and stone circles were built at such places, and may have been used to contain and increase the current. Some of these intersection points have been the sites of repeated accidents or hauntings. One such place is Windsor Park in England, where Herne the Hunter, horned god of the witches, has been seen several times, and other unusual events have taken place. It seems that the energy disturbance around the leys causes the veil between this world and that of the spirits to tremble and sometimes tear. Interest in ghosts, old buildings and local legends are part of investigating earth mysteries.

Ley lines warrant serious study in themselves, and many books have been written about them. No one really understands the energy that follows these lines, but its existence is widely accepted. It is possible to investigate such energies by dowsing, and we shall be looking at this in our Practice section at the end of the chapter.

Seasons and sexuality

The earth has seasons, and people living far from the equator noticed how the approach and retreat of the sun related to the fertility of their Mother. Many ancient structures mark the cycle of the divine mating of the earth and sun. For instance, the long barrow at Stoney Littleton in the English Cotswolds is shaped so that every year, for a few moments on Midwinter's day, the sun shines right through to the end of the long passage at the centre of the barrow. This passage has been likened to a vagina, and there is a natural cup mark on a special stone that is illuminated by the penetrating rays. This barrow has many special spiral-shaped fossils, no doubt chosen for their symbolic meaning. Most ancient sites such as this were also burial places, but to suggest that they were merely tombs is as foolish as to say that churches are 'tombs' because bodies are buried there. These places were sacred to the Mother and the dead were returned to the holy earth, to the tomb that was also womb, so that one day they would be reborn.

Many structures seem to honour the sexuality of Mother Earth. Glastonbury Tor in Somerset looks like a pregnant belly, and Silbury Hill in Wiltshire, erected c 2750 BCE (Before Common Era), has been likened to a breast and a swollen belly. However, Shuttle and Redgrove in *The Wise Wound* (Harper Collins, 1994) equate such shapes with the rounded neck of the womb which '... resembles the tumulus, and we interpret this as the return of the dead to await resurrection through the cervix of the earth-mother'. Speaking of stone circles they continue, 'It is possible that Stonehenge and Avebury and the whole complex of Neolithic monuments ... were computers of ... sophistication that were used to establish ... the movements of the sun and moon.'

So we have sites honouring the secret and fertile places of the female body, the body of the earth, and we have sites linking earth and sky in celebration. We also have structures to calculate precisely the relationship of the sun, moon, earth and other planets and stars. It seems evident that the ancients perceived links between many things: the sexual and spiritual, life and death, land and sky, the energies within the earth, and within man himself and the distant stars, from which our ancestors may have come. They may have built their temples of soil and stone to conjure the return of the sun in winter's depth, to access earth energies, to increase fertility, to ensure rebirth for self and kinsmen or to communicate in some way with people from the stars. It may have been all of these at different times, and more. The ancients percieved things that we have lost; they had a holistic perception. Seeing with the eye of the mystic, they lived on a different level, in a different relationship to the earth. They had direct knowledge of forces that we can no longer appreciate.

LeFT AND RIGHT BRAIN

In *The Origin of Consciousness in the Breakdown of the Bicameral Mind* (1976) Julian Jaynes suggests that ancient man possessed a bicameral mind in which the temporal lobes of the brain were interconnected across the anterior commissure between the two hemispheres. So these people would have heard 'voices' like a schizophrenic does and would have been driven to take actions accordingly. The heroes in the Greek myths, he says, heard the 'voices of the Gods' in their heads. It is well known today that the right and left hemispheres of the brain perform different functions. The right brain relates to the left side of the body and (in right-handed people) it thinks intuitively, whereas the left brain thinks logically and relates to the right side of the body. The reverse is true for left-handed people.

Jaynes suggests that the ability to 'hear' voices was lost abruptly by most people at more or less the same time, so people would have felt that the gods had abandoned them. Those who retained the ability to 'hear' would then have been sought out as soothsayers. However, the loss of the voices would have resulted in the desertion of the sacred sites where the skulls of the ancestors housed wisdom, and the voices had spoken most 'ringingly'. This concept is explored by Danny Sullivan in the article 'Talking Heads', published in *Third Stone* magazine, Midsummer 1995.

Today we are largely stranded in the side of our brain that thinks with structure and logic, cut off from the gifts of the other side – instinct, inspiration and mystical knowing, although we still possess them. Special sites of antiquity have the power to revive our split consciousness and give us a vivid experience of the oneness of human, earth and sky. This is very relevant to the modern pagan, in search of connections with her/his roots and a true experience of the divine in nature – an intense and real participation that makes one know one is 'home'. One of the goals of modern pagans is often to find ways of revitalising this 'older' knowledge and reconnecting with it.

Many ways may be sought – through trance, dream, shamanic experience or even drugs. However, the best way is to look for this 'knowing' at its source – in Nature herself. Contact with the earth energies can be made at any place of natural beauty, but numbers of pagans regularly visit ancient sites because these sites are where the power may be most strongly felt, as we shall see.

A sense of place

A visit to the White Horse at Uffington

There are several white horses etched upon the English hills. Most of them are fairly recent – although they may be updates of older figures, but the White Horse at Uffington, Oxfordshire, is very old, possibly dating back to 1400 BCE. Interestingly, it is seen far better from the air, suggesting communication with travellers from the skies.

White Horse, Uffington

The earth energy of the ley lines has been linked to dragons or great serpents. Tales of mythical creatures may be personifications of earth forces. The Uffington White Horse does not look like a horse. There is something serpentine about its long body and small head.

. . . The air freshened as we climbed the slope. Although steep, the way seemed easy and I was aware of increasing energy the higher we went. Soon we came to the summit, near the head of the horse. A sign told us not to walk on the horse, as too many tramping feet would wear away the ancient structure. However, I knew I just had to stand within the head of the great horse. Taking off my shoes I tiptoed over the grass and stood close to the eye, facing north.

Ahead of me the hills billowed into the horizon, and the wind swept the hair from my shoulders. But I was aware of something else – something surging, heaving and rolling, a great tide of power gushing from the north through the landscape and through me as it cascaded inexorably onwards. It was like the coils of a serpent looping vertically as it moved over the hills, it was like the beat of a huge heart, pounding an unseen flow through the earth and through me, for I was part of this exultant tide.

From the north I turned through east, south, west and back to the north, conjuring the four elements of Earth, Air, Fire and Water in turn. Now within my Temple of the Winds I was even more powerfully aware of the energy current. It filled me with joy, it seemed to dissolve the boundaries of my being so I could participate fully in this great, unending belly-laugh of the hills. With starlight vision I saw the inexpressible – it seemed as if strands of my hair trailed into the Milky Way. I wanted to dance, jump and call out, but instead I lay down on the ground, legs towards the north and rode on the current for a while. Then I stood up and placed my palms on the horse's eye. The sun lanced down through my hands into the eye and I felt a surge of personal energy. I knew my experience was complete. Slowly I circled through north, east, south and west, and emerged, walking gently from the horse's head, as I had come . . .

This was a personal perception of earth energy. The experience, vivid and unforgettable, had the gift of 'connecting' me. You cannot lose your sense of meaning in the light of such things, for it is all around. This can be felt at all times, but the Uffington White Horse brought it to me in its full splendour. Later I looked up data on ley lines near the White Horse and found that one runs almost exactly in the direction I was facing, but it passes through Dragon Hill, which is slightly to the west of the Horse. No one is sure how broad leys are. They may be the breadth of a track or much wider. Was the energy I felt ley energy? I'm inclined to think it was.

Such experiences at important sites are not uncommon for those who seek them. They may take the form of visions seen with the inner sight. I know of others who have had contact with extra-terrestials in such places. Of course responses can be much less dramatic: you may simply feel energised and cheered. A good experience can set you up for weeks, making you feel positive and happy. These feelings are available to anybody – it's just a matter of opening your eyes. They are the stuff of pagan spirituality and important to the pagan world view.

Of course, not all visits are so significant. Sometimes it may feel quite dead; at others there is interference. When I visited a stone circle not many miles from the White Horse at Uffington I found that entry now has to be paid for and the ancient stones are policed. Wishing to escape from this I left the circle for the shelter of the surrounding trees only to be followed by the caretaker who asked me if I intended to go to the toilet! A sense of humour came in handy at that point, but poems and visions? Forget it!

Developing earth awareness

Visit ancient sites at times when they are unlikely to be crowded, and go with a relaxed and open mind. Go to enjoy yourself. Take a picnic if you like. Simply notice your surroundings, smells and sounds as well as sights. How is the place affecting your mood? Are you uplifted, pleased – or bored? Pick up any interesting stones or bits of wood you may find – it doesn't matter why they are interesting, don't talk yourself out of anything and don't look for something that's esoteric or symbolic. Be playful. Take a real interest in your locality – buildings, woodlands, local stories, reported hauntings. Investigate where you can.

Get yourself a special notebook to record where you go, how you feel and the dates. After some months of regular visits, either to the same site or different ones you may find a pattern emerges. Don't forget to record the phase of the moon when you visit – this is shown in many diaries and calendars. Is she waxing, full or waning? After a while you may find a connection between the phase and how you feel, for the moon's phases form an energy tide on the earth, in some ways similar to the effects of her gravity on the seas. If you wish it to be, this notebook can form a record of the development of your earth awareness. If you live outside the British Isles and there are no obvious sacred sites available, you will have to find ones of your own. Any place that feels special to you is worth exploring.

NB Always use common sense when visiting special sites. Never denude or deface the site or plant life; don't take archaeological remains found with a metal detector (for in so doing you are depriving us all of our heritage); leave no litter, not even the remains of a joss stick.

PRACTICE

One invaluable aid in developing earth awareness is dowsing. This is more than just a method of finding water with a hazel twig that twitches when a spring is underfoot. It can reveal energy currents, and sometimes the energies are strong in ancient sites. You may dowse with a pendulum. It is best to do this with a small piece of crystal suspended on a chain, that you keep just for this purpose. Simply relax, support your arm and dangle your pendulum over the area. Clockwise movement usually indicates positive energy, anticlockwise negative energy. Programme your pendulum before you start by asking yes/no questions to which you know the answer, and noting in which direction it moves. If the pendulum doesn't move, don't give up. Move to a different location and try again. Anyone can do this. Eventually your pendulum will start to move. Make a note of where and how, and look for patterns.

I'm a recent convert to dowsing rods and these seem easier than
a pendulum. You can make dowsing rods from a wire coat
hanger. You will need two rods, bent in a right angle, with an
upright of about 12cm, that you hold, and a length of about
27cm that you poke out in front of you. Hold the short ends
loosely in your fists, elbows at your sides, arms bent so your fists
are at chest level. You can walk around your chosen site and plot
the energy fluctuations. The rods will move – sometimes
clockwise, sometimes anticlockwise. Experiment for yourself.
Keeping to where the energies are strongest, you can trace lines
of energy on the land. Americans may need to be careful,
however, for dowsing is illegal in some states, so you may have
to rely on developing your instincts. Whatever the case, good
hunting!

Further information

Bord, Janet and Colin, *Mysterious Britain*, Paladin, 1974

—— *The Secret Country*, Book Club Ass./Paul Elek, 1976

Devereux, Paul, and Thomson, Ian, *The Ley Hunter's Companion*,
Thames & Hudson, 1979

—— *Symbolic Landscapes*, Gothic Image, 1992

Jones, Kathy, *The Ancient British Goddess*, Ariadne, 1991

—— *Spinning the Wheel of Ana*, Ariadne, 1994

Nielsen, Greg, and Polansky, Joseph, *Pendulum Power*, Aquarian,
1986

Wilson, Colin, *Starseekers*, Granada, 1982 – not specifically 'earth
mysteries' but he makes interesting points about man's
consciousness.

3rd Stone Magazine Earth mysteries magazine with a Cotswold bias.
SAE to PO Box 258, Cheltenham GL53 0HR, UK. Sample issue
£2.50 at time of writing.

GODDESS AND GOD

A foolish consistency is the hobgoblin of little minds
Ralph Waldo Emerson

The Goddess has been recently rediscovered, giving a different perspective on history, society and the role of the sexes. She offers healing through the celebration of the body mysteries, through feminine knowledge, intuition, creativity, fierceness and caring. The Goddess is the single most potent force in paganism, transforming our ideas of role-models and power – for the Goddess is certainly not a transvestite God. By honouring the feminine, new ways can be found to respect the earth and humanity, and important experiences such as birth, pregnancy, sex, death and menstruation. This radical shift in values is needed to make sense of our experience, and even to survive as a species.

The God is the life-force that surges outwards, that impregnates. He is the Guardian and Carer, and is gentle, wise and savage. He stands as Protector to the Goddess and Her creations and is neither law-giver nor judge. The Goddess can inspire women to discover their power. She can also inspire men to find their gentle side and so connect with the playful, lusty, strong and tender person of the God.

However, pagans may see Goddess, God and gods in different ways. Sometimes it may seem there is only One, asexual, all-pervasive divine presence. At others we may sense many goddesses and gods, some within us, some outside, enhancing our ability to live, experience and be creative. It is not a question of what is 'true' in some crystallised fashion, but of what is useful, meaningful and beautiful.

The Goddess is usually seen as synonymous with Mother Earth, and her consort is the Horned God. Belief in a Goddess probably originated with palaeolithic hunter-gathers at a time when the male role in procreation was not appreciated. To pagans the Goddess is 'first', but this does not mean superior: in this context it is more about the order of thinking. However, some pagans find that a dedication to the Goddess alone is sufficient for spiritual meaning.

An awareness of lunar phases, waxing, full and waning, led to the concept of a Triple Goddess, Maiden, Mother and Crone. The idea of the God may have come later. He was seen as the embodiment of potency and fertility and yet as the bringer of death and entry into the Hidden. However, this is only part of the story: the pagan view of god-within-matter includes animism, pantheism and polytheism.

Animism means seeing all things as alive. This is the magical world in which stones have personalities and streams speak to us, which tends to be left behind in childhood. Pantheism is the belief that God is everywhere, and amounts almost to the same thing, but with a more pronounced sense of deity. Polytheism means there are many gods, for they are needed to express the lavish miscellany of life. Shan defines this succinctly: 'Animism means "all is alive", pantheism means "all is god" and polytheism means "many gods"'. Existence is diverse, the gods are existence and therefore varied. After all, the most fertile ground produces the richest variety of wildflowers, trees, bushes and all the butterflies and bees to flutter and buzz in them. Pagans see religion in the same way.

fORMS Of the DIVINE

Pagan pantheons display colourful parades of divinities: joyful, fearful, tragic, funny and often breathtakingly beautiful. They offer us inspiring images that may stimulate creativity in poetry, painting and dance, or may dramatise aspects of ourselves. Myths are often allegories for internal experience and pagans borrow from the Celts, Greeks, Romans and others. Here we look at a few, but anyone interested can look farther, and a quest to find your own goddesses and gods is a true 'magical mystery tour'.

Diana and Aradia

Aradia is especially important to Wiccans, and C. G. Leland's *Aradia, Gospel of the Witches* is one of the key sources of the current Wicca/witchcraft revival. It tells us: 'Diana was the first created before all creation; in her were all things; out of herself, the first darkness she divided herself; into darkness and light she was divided. Lucifer, her brother and son, herself and her other half, was the light.'

The story continues with details of how Diana fell in love with Lucifer and seduced him, how she became mistress of all sorcery and how her union with her brother produced a daughter, Aradia. Aradia then became her emissary upon earth, bringing knowledge of witchcraft and hidden arts to the poor and deprived. Aradia says: 'My mother will teach you all things and ye shall be freed from slavery.'

Whether we are enslaved by materialism, dogma, inhibitions or prohibitions, this is an exciting message and Wiccans have preserved it in their ceremonies. Aradia, who is linked to the full moon, brings wisdom, the starlight vision, and freedom – she is a female Messiah. She also represents delight in the pleasures of the flesh and whispers of secret worship in grove and on moonlit hill. Young, beautiful and wise she is the counterpart of the horned god Cernunnos, a true Nature Goddess of the Witches.

The story of Diana as primal Mother Goddess, giving birth to her son/consort is only one of many from different mythologies and cultures. It is symbolic and certainly does not imply any belief in or respect for incest.

Lucifer (meaning Light) is well known as the archangel who succumbed to pride and was thrown out of heaven to become the Devil. However, the Lucifer in this story is a different matter entirely and no one should infer from it that Wiccans worship the Devil, for they certainly do not; in fact they do not believe in him.

ĐERNE TĐE ĐUNTER/CERNUNNOS

These are the names of the Wiccan Horned God. His horns have many meanings: they are a testimony of animal vitality and potency, they signify crescent moons, and they represent the fallopian tubes that link the ovaries to the womb. In Shakespeare's time 'wearing the horns' was a sign of the cuckold, a man whose wife was unfaithful. Pagans see this differently, for by identifying with the sexuality of his mate a man can achieve greater fulfilment for himself and draw closer to the Goddess. The horns are a proud and glorious declaration of revelry in the pleasures of the body. It seems the Horned God was later debased as the Christian Devil, but there is nothing evil about him: he is protective, wise and merry.

The Horned God is the Nature God, eternally slain in bull and stag, yet eternally reborn to be hunted anew. He is also the Hunter, for to identify with his prey, Stone Age man may well have donned a 'crown' of horns, so hunter and hunted became one in a mystical duo.

Cernunnos is the Celtic version of the Horned God, but is probably Latinised, and may have come from the same source as Herne, in British folklore. Herne leads the Wild Hunt across the sky. This is a tempestuous spirit cavalcade, a true personification of lawless nature. There are various legends attached to it, one of which concerns Windsor Great Park, in England, where it is said to appear at times of national crisis. It has also been said that witches used to impersonate the wild hunt to frighten possible captors!

Persephone and Demeter

This is a well-known Greek myth about another mother and daughter duo. It is the story of the rape of innocent Persephone by the underworld god Pluto (Hades to the Greeks). Her mother Demeter is goddess of nature, and after her daughter's abduction she goes into mourning and eternal winter claims the land. All the other gods are disturbed by this and so it is agreed that Persephone will live above ground for half of the year. She cannot leave Pluto's kingdom permanently, because while there she has eaten some pomegranate seeds. For four months she must return to the land of darkness, while her mother mourns anew and winter reigns. Spring comes again when Persephone re-emerges.

Many people now believe that this myth should not be interpreted in terms of female freedom being taken away by male force, or of the seasons being determined by brutal rape. A closer look tells a different tale. The pomegranate is a symbol of fertility, and Pluto, as god of the land beneath the earth, is in a sense sent by the Great Mother herself. Astrologically Pluto rules the feminine sign of Scorpio, and is associated with power, sexuality, death, rebirth and transformation. What takes Persephone by storm is the onset of mature sexuality, for sexuality brings direct experience of the awesome power of nature as it manifests in tempest, earthquake and tropical sun. It also has links with karma. Sexuality is knowledge, knowledge is power – Persephone becomes Queen of the Underworld – and power means change.

Persephone is also called Kore, and her worship was important in the rites of Eleusis, the mystery cult. This is a myth of many meanings, one of which is initiation, which means entry into a new understanding – a concept worthy of our consideration.

Pan

The 'goat-foot god' exemplifies nature at its wildest and most unpredictable, and indeed he is another horned god. One of the myths about Pan concerns his love for the nymph Syrinx, who, in common with most of his lovers found him a bit much. The river god who was Syrinx's father turned her into a reed to save her from him. Pan – obviously a pragmatist – plucked the reed and made his Pan-pipes. This is a haunting tale of loss inspiring creativity, and of participation. Pan does not walk away in mourning from the riverside; nor does he pick the reed and set it on a shrine. Instead he makes something of it. The story has a lot to tell us about how to deal with frustration, and about connecting with nature and truth.

The word 'panic' derives from his name, and may be allied to that strange and overwhelming fear that can take possession when we are totally alone with nature, on a mountain or deserted moor. This is no human fear. The very soil murmurs of a primeval power that hardly notices our existence. However, in psychotheraputic terms panic and hysteria can have their roots in disconnection from feeling. Fear of nature can be a result of feeling separated from her. Mysticism is one way of reuniting. Working up a healthy sweat through a hard slog up a hill, or simply putting palms to the earth can work too. Chaotic and orgiastic, Pan tells us to surrender to the natural in order to understand better, to feel better.

Pan also means 'all', which perhaps implies that Pan is omnipresent. Plutarch tells the story of a sailor passing the Echinades Islands at the time Christianity was beginning to take over much of the known world. This sailor heard a voice crying 'Great Pan is dead'. To pagans that has a poignant ring. However, Great Pan is now very much reincarnated, and he represents the 'all-ness' without dogma that somehow unites pagans across the globe.

Isis

This Egyptian goddess, whose worship spread far afield, has been described as the most complete goddess form that has evolved. Her very name evokes the archetypal Feminine. She and her husband Osiris ruled Egypt and taught mankind the skills of civilisation, but their brother Set became jealous and killed Osiris. However, Isis searched for all the parts of the dismembered body, and magically conceived a child, the god Horus, from her dead husband. Osiris became king of the Underworld, but he is really one of many dying and resurrecting vegetation gods, reborn as his son Horus.

So Isis was the faithful wife and mother who understood suffering. She was also goddess of magic and healing, in which she was helped by Thoth, god of wisdom, showing that true feeling allied to understanding is the basis of magical endeavour. Thoth was married to Ma'at, who represents the inescapable order of the cosmos – yet another factor for the magician/witch striving to act in harmony with Nature and to understand it better.

Mercury/Hermes

Hermes was the messenger of the Olympian gods, called Mercury by the Romans and pictured wearing winged sandals. He was the god of intellect, and of travel and trade. One of his most important functions was to lead dead souls into Hades, and in that he was unique for very few could enter the dark realms and return. This suggests the way in that intellect can lead us to hidden wisdom. He was also something of a trickster, being patron of thieves, and he had many lovers – there has even been a suggestion that his identity is not strictly masculine, and that he is more androgynous. However, as god of the intellect and the swift retort he is 'airy', and we associate the element of air with masculinity.

Mercury carries a staff, called a caduceus, around which serpents are entwined. Serpents represent wisdom and sexuality, among other meanings, so this is no simple god. As the father of Pan he represents the cerebral leading to the instinctual. Conversely, the instinctual may be a valid path to understanding.

Cerridwen

This is a Welsh goddess, well known for her cauldron of inspiration and rebirth, from which the bodies of dead heroes emerged, healed and alive. Often she is seen as the Dark Mother, the tomb that swallows, and one of her symbols was the sow. She had a hideous son called Afagddu, which means Darkness, and for him she prepared a brew of wisdom. However, a few drops of this spilt onto little Gwion, whom she asked to stir it, and he sucked the splashes and received the gift of wisdom. There follows a chase in which Cerridwen and Gwion assume many different animal forms until at last he becomes a grain of wheat and she becomes a hen and eats him. Subsequently she gives birth to a beautiful boy who is the bard Taliesin, of legendary fame. The message from this is that from death comes life, from darkness comes beauty, and from the unnameable comes wisdom. It is an initiation story.

Lugh

This is the Irish sun god, or god of light – his name means 'shining one'. He was also god of many crafts. He is celebrated especially at Lughnasadh, or Lammas, the festival at the beginning of August. At this time the god is cut down and is reborn in the bread made from the harvest grains, so identifying with the sun, which 'dies' and 'resurrects' in temperate latitudes. Because of this he can also be seen as a vegetation god, for plants come and go with the sun.

Brigid/Bride

Bride (pronounced *Breed*) is the great mother goddess of Ireland, and is often seen as a form of the Triple Goddess. She was widely worshipped and was particularly goddess of fire, smithcraft, healing, childbirth and poetic inspiration. As St Bridget, she is beloved of the Irish, who have made many wells sacred to her. It seems that expanding Christianity turned as many heathen customs as possible into Christian ones, and Bride survived as Ireland's favourite female saint. The symbol for Bridget is the woven Bridget's cross, which is a type of cross where the four arms meet to form a square centre and opposite arms are parallel but do not form a straight line. This can be seen as a fire wheel, but it is also like a swastika. The cross has many meanings which have nothing to do with Christianity, and the swastika has occult significance that pre-dates the Nazis by

Green Man

centuries. One of the interpretations of the swastika is that it consists of four gammas, or Greek 'g's (the Russian 'g' is similar) and so is the initial of Gaia, the Greek Earth Mother written four times, so meaning fecundity.

The Green Man

I include the Green Man here because he seems quintessentially pagan. His image is found on many churches as the 'foliate mask' – a face made up of leaves. The Green Man is also embodied in the Green Knight of Arthurian legend. The Green Knight represents nature, and more specifically the Holly King, or King of the Waning Year, from midsummer to Yule, while Gawain was the Oak King of the Waxing Year. Barely even human, he has a vegetation face, sometimes benevolent yet strangely remorseless. He appears in church architecture, perhaps placed there by masons who weren't as Christian as they pretended. Along with the Sheil-na-Gig, the hag with the yawning vulva, also found in churches (notably at Kilpeck Church, in Herefordshire), he is a reminder of the ineradicability of pagan feeling, and he can be seen each time we are in woods and look up at the sunlight through a roof of woven leaves.

Practice

We have examined a small number of goddesses and gods, but most areas of human life are represented. Are you undergoing deep and unsettling changes? Persephone or Cerridwen can help. Do you need clear thought for a project, interview or exam? This is Mercury's province. If you need help in love, call on great Isis. Perhaps you need help in creative endeavours, conception, childbirth: put this in the hands of Brigid. Need healing, energy, freedom from care? Call on Cernunnos or the Green Man. Pan is best left to his work of attending nature, for his energies are unpredictable.

Settle yourself quietly, out of doors if possible, in a place where you will feel safe and will not be interrupted. Still your mind and allow a feeling of peace to bathe you. Close your eyes and visualise the god or goddess of your need approaching you, tell him or her your trouble and put it in her/his hands. Allow yourself to feel consoled and optimistic. The Great Ones are there to help humans. When you have finished, thank your god/dess, take a deep breath and open your eyes. Place your palms on the ground for a few seconds to earth yourself. Make a small offering to the deity – perhaps some food or wine placed upon the earth, and know that your pleas will be attended to.

Perhaps you would like to choose one of the familiar pantheons, Celts, Graeco-Roman or Egyptian and explore further for yourself. What gods or goddesses really inspire you? And why?

Further information

Baring, Anne, and Cashford, Jules, *Myth of the Goddess*, Penguin, 1993

Cotterell, Arthur, *A Dictionary of World Mythology*, Oxford, 1986

Farrar, Janet and Stewart, *The Witches' Goddess*, Phoenix, 1987

–––––– *The Witches' God*, Phoenix, 1989

Jones, G. and T. (trans.), *The Mabinogion* (Welsh myths), Dent, 1989

There is a host of colourful books available on the gods of Greece and Rome, Celtic gods, Norse gods, Egyptian gods and others. Choose what appeals to you from bookshops and libraries. Often books aimed at older children tell the stories beautifully and are better than adult works, which may be rather scholarly. Roger Lancelyn Green (Penguin Classics) is good on this.

WITCHCRAFT
AND WICCA

... our Goddess ever inclineth to love and mirth and happiness: and guardeth and cherisheth Her hidden children in life, and in death

From the Second Legend of the Goddess

What is Witchcraft?

Witchcraft is a religion of nature and goddess worship that celebrates the cycles of the seasons in eight festivals or Sabbats. In these the mysteries of birth, sex and death and the rhythms of growth and decay of the natural world are honoured. To a great extent witchcraft is a fertility cult. Today we are not so worried about crop yield and young animals, but we are concerned with the welfare of our children and with other creative meanings. Our link with the earth is just as important as ever, and needs to be reaffirmed. Witches also worship the God, consort of the Goddess, and are inspired by many ancient myths: principally Celtic but also Greek, Egyptian and others. Wicca, a major witchcraft tradition, is probably the most structured form of paganism today. Witchcraft is both a religion and a magical system.

Many pagans perform magic of some sort because it is a natural product of being in harmony with the forces of nature. There is nothing supernatural about this. It is a matter of visualising, creating a clear inner picture of what you require, raising power by dancing or chanting, and using ritual as external activity, to focus and ground. One of the effects of ritual is to still the workings and worryings of the conscious mind so that the older wisdom of the unconscious may take effect. Magic has the effect of raising the consciousness and exalting the human spirit, and that is often more important than the goal of the spell. Most spells are to heal a person or the environment. For a fuller discussion of magic and its meanings read *Witchcraft – a beginner's guide* in this series.

There is some confusion about the terms 'Wiccan' and 'witch', so for simplicity I will divide Wiccans/witches into four main types.

Traditional

Some witches call themselves 'traditional' because they follow ways that have been passed down through the family. However, it also seems that much 'traditional' witchcraft is less of a religion and more a set of customs that may not be called witchcraft by those who follow them – times of persecution would doubtless have had an effect.

Hedge witches

These are lone witches, who usually celebrate the eight Sabbats and each Full Moon, following a path similar to Wicca, but more spontaneous. Variations may be immense, as solo witches are often visionary, poetical and interested in self-development. They are not bound by any rules except 'harm none' which is almost universal. Solo witches are often called 'hedge witches', but there is a trend, especially in America, to call lone witchcraft 'Wicca'. Witches of this sort are often motivated by visions and glean information from books. They initiate or 'dedicate' themselves when they wish, usually practise magic, have no degree system, keep their own records, or not, as they wish, and may honour the Goddess more strongly, or possibly the God.

OPEN-STYLE CRAFT

There are less formal groupings of witches, who also work alone. They have many other names, such as Kitchen Magic, Folk Magic, the Craft or Weavers. Although they may not see themselves as part of the same group, there are many similarities. They are independent and strongly feminist. Sometimes there may be a defined leader, usually a priestess, or a couple. Sometimes they form groups/covens or circles but tend to be informal about it and also work alone. There is an emphasis on personal development, intuition, shamanic techniques, practical crafts, ecology and healing. It is this more open style which has created courses, public festivals and a developing sense of pagan community and available services.

WICCANS

These have a defined system of initiation and group in covens under a High Priestess and High Priest. It is a mystery tradition that follows definite rules for festivals and rituals, celebrating eight yearly sabbats, and esbats usually at Full Moon. Wiccans also call themselves 'witches' and Wicca is often referred to as 'the Craft'. Wicca has existed in its present form since the 1940s and rites and ceremonies are recorded in a 'Book of Shadows' and copied down by initiates as part of their training.

In practice these four types can overlap a great deal and none is really more authentic than the other. However, to give a starting-point, the following concentrates on Wicca, as it is currently the most structured form.

Being also a magical system, Wiccan rites take place within a magic circle. This is a circle created by visualisation and ritual, that exists on the spirit plane and offers protection and containment. Covens do magic at the Sabbats, or at other times. At no time is anything intended to harm, for the one rule that Wiccans and witches follow regarding all activity – not just magical – is 'If it harms none, do what you will'.

Wiccan covens are not self-development groups, but ways are offered to expand as a person. Training nights are an important routine, and one is expected to be discreet about the identity of other members. Wicca is a mystery religion akin to those of much earlier times and there are secrets that are not shared with outsiders. The details of initiation rites are not discussed in advance and this can make the experience more powerful. However, the real mystery is what happens inside, which is incommunicable. Rites can unlock hidden depths and bring about an inner change, even if what happens outwardly is less than majestic. The transcendent is approached through the body, not by denying it – the pagan approach – and so Wiccans usually regard having fun as important. Feasting is part of the process and coven members will often bring food to enjoy after the ritual.

The High Priestess is really the coven leader. She is 'first among equals' but that should not mean 'superior' in the usual sense. Goddess-worship and the full development of female potential are very basic to the ideals of the Craft. Rites are often conducted 'sky-clad' which means in the nude, but sexual exploitation is absolutely forbidden and no one under 18 is initiated.

First of all, newcomers are accepted into covens as 'neophytes' or novices. As they progress they are initiated into the First Degree. This is followed by the Second and Third Degree, after which they are regarded as being in a position to leave, form their own covens and initiate others. Initiation involves certain vows of support, but these are not binding in any compulsive fashion. Covens can really be of any number that remains sufficiently cosy and each initiate is considered to be Priestess or Priest of the Goddess – no one has the exclusive hot line to the divine. Covens are not cults and anyone may leave when they wish. However, it is common sense to approach any new group of people with care and ensure that you feel comfortable before committing yourself. Wiccans do not seek converts for there is nothing evangelical about the religion. In Wicca the focus is, to a great extent, the Sacred Marriage of Goddess and God. Following on from this, Druidry emphasises the birth of the Divine Child. There are many connections between the two paths that are being rediscovered by present-day pagans.

The history of Wicca

Wiccans feel their ancestry begins back in the days of standing stone and tumulus, when the great Earth Mother was universally worshipped. By 500 BCE the Celts had become a major force in Europe. Women were powerful in their society. They have passed down to us the four main festivals of Imbolc, Beltane, Lammas and Samhain that we shall be looking at later.

European influences

Two strands of thought from Europe were also influential. The cult of Apollo emphasised philosophy, consciousness and solar rites (Apollo was a Sun god). On the other hand the Dionysian approach was one of ecstacy, trance and merging – more a province of the grove than the temple. Dionysus was god of wine and has been associated with the intuitive water sign, Pisces. Both of these ways were to some extent combined in the mystery cults of Isis and Eleusis, which aimed to raise consciousness through philosophy and inspirational experience.

Persecution

Mostly the ancient gods lived comfortably side by side until Christianity appeared, proclaiming itself the one and only truth and stamping out competition with a savage ruthlessness on the part of some churchmen. The old religions disappeared or went underground. Then the Renaissance saw a growth in ritual magic, which in a sense was a revival of the Apollonian approach. However, these magicians had rites that called upon an ostentatious array of saints so they mostly evaded persecution. Magicians were often influential men.

The Dionysian strand lived on in village witches, and it was upon these that the inquisition heaped its wrath. Most of its victims were women, and there may have been as many as nine million of them, throughout the Middle Ages. Witches were tortured horrifically and burnt at the stake – alive, if they refused to admit what their captors wished – which must have put many unfortunates in a no-win situation. After the Reformation this was illegal in England (but not in Scotland) and witches were hanged instead. It is said that the persecutors would not have caught a real witch, but this is uncertain. Any 'real' witches would have scented trouble a mile off, but escape may not always have been practical, especially if one was loyal to the community.

TOLERANCE

Easier times approached and interest in the occult grew in the nineteenth century, which also produced a work by Charles Leland called *Aradia, or The Gospel of the Witches* (the Vangelo). Leland was a charismatic and urbane man who gained entry to societies normally suspicious of outsiders. *Aradia* tells of secret rites to the Goddess Diana and Aradia, her daughter: this was called the Old Religion, and had been handed down through many centuries. The Vangelo forms the basis of some of the Wiccan rites of today and Wicca/witchcraft is still called the Old Religion.

Next came the lively and well-travelled Margaret Murray, an anthropologist and Egyptologist whose studies revealed the existence of an extensive witch-cult and the involvement of the English monarchy in this. In the early twentieth century she published *The Witch Cult in Western Europe, The God of the Witches* and later *The Divine King in England*.

Gerald Gardner, who may be regarded as the founder of modern Wicca, was initiated into a traditional witch coven in the New Forest. He is also said to have had connections with an East Anglian coven of a similar nature, led by a colourful 'cunning man' called George Pickingill. Gardner was heavily criticised for publicising witchcraft but he said he wished to make it available to younger people who could revitalise the old ways and pass them on.

Aleister Crowley, better known as 'the Beast' and sometimes thought of as a black magician, also had links with Pickingill. Crowley was probably a tormented character, whose habits (such as relieving himself upon the floor of his hostess's lounge!) suggest he had more than a little of the rebellious toddler about him. His evil reputation is not really justified, and he coined some wise sayings, notably 'Do what thou wilt shall be the whole of the law; Love is the Law, Love under Will'. The 'True Will' is not the desires of the ego, and the role of love is supportive, not subordinate.

The last historical figure was Alex Sanders, whose initiation history is obscure. His grandmother may have introduced him into traditional witchcraft, or he may have entered a Gardnerian coven. At all events, the strand of Wicca that we know today as 'Alexandrian' comes from him, whereas the 'Gardnerian' originates with Gerald Gardner. The differences between them are not extreme and we shall not be concerning ourselves with them here.

This is the story of modern Wicca, originating in an unbroken line from the Stone Age, through the Celts and Greeks, surviving underground in cults and covens through the 'Burning Times'. It was resurrected almost intact by recent scholars, and tidied up by Gerald Gardner and Alex Sanders to be practised by us today.

Myth and history

However, almost everything written about above has been contested, some of it very hotly. Leland was a satirist and the *Vangelo* has been called a hoax. Margaret Murray has been called a deluded old woman and Gardner has been accused of borrowing wildly from every source under the sun. Some say there never was a universal Goddess worship and the 'witch-cult' was an invention of a Church that wanted scapegoats. So what are we to believe?

The truth is probably somewhere in between. There may never have been universal Goddess worship but there have been more female figures unearthed in digs than male ones, and it seems women undoubtedly held real power in Celtic society. As for the Middle Ages, it seems true that the patriarchal organisation of the Church, influenced by the woman-hating St Paul, denied space to many things that are considered feminine – the instinctual, the non-rational and indeed the naturally physical. It also called evil any form of worship other than its own. Life in those times was very hard. Goddess worship, far from condemning bodily enjoyment as sinful, actually regarded it as a divine gift. It seems reasonable that this, along with such things as ecstatic experience and herbal lore, may have been secretly preserved by the common people, mostly in a disorganised form, and sometimes called by other names than 'witchcraft'.

Further, Margaret Murray appears to have been a lucid and scholarly lady and Leland a sensitive and poetical man. There seems little reason for him to invent the *Vangelo* and in any case the mixed mythology that it contains is rather what one would expect of a doctrine kept secretly alive for many years by an illiterate and oppressed peasantry. In respect of Gerald Gardner and Alex Sanders, regardless of their origins the contribution they have made is undeniable and inspiring. If Wiccans and witches have to invent stories – and many do – perhaps it is an indictment of our society that intuitive people feel they have to invent 'authentic' sources to be accepted.

All this is useful because it is the Wiccan 'myth' and has been much debated. Whatever may be true, what we practise now cannot be the same as the ancient ways of cave, grove and stone circle. Nor should it be, for we and our needs are very different from our ancestors. The literal truth is not really important, especially to pagans, because paganism is not about doctrine or dogma, but what fires the imagination, frees the soul and brings the kinship of the heart. Witchcraft is a way of beauty and inspiration, where there is poetry in leaf and stone, wisdom in the hills and freedom for the spirit, where the Old Ones walk with us and each small pleasure is a festival. Most people initiated as Wiccans or witches feel they have come home. It is a feeling of comfort but also of a strange and terrible awe. For what we come 'home' to is very old indeed – older even than humanity itself.

PRACTICE

You may like to do some historical research yourself. The 'Further Reading' for this chapter offers suggestions.

More importantly, go out by yourself into a forest or lonely field and try to imagine what it was like to be a poor person in medieval times, or before. There is no central heating to shield you from winter's blast. Perhaps you have not even a candle to light after the sun has set. Your crops are at the mercy of the weather and inconvenient rain could mean a long, hungry time for yourself and those you care for. If you break a leg on the way home there will be no anaesthetic or welcoming hospital to help you. Likewise, if you or a loved one expect a baby the birth will take place on a pile of rushes or coarse cloth – and you must hope against hope that there will be no complications.

What might your ideas about the gods be? To whom would you turn for help? What might you do to feel better about life, more hopeful? Make a note of all thoughts, however far-fetched they may seem.

Further information

Beth, Rae, *Hedgewitch - A Guide to Solitary Witchcraft*, Hale 1994

Cohn, Norman, *Europe's Inner Demons*, New York Basic Books, 1975

Crowley, Vivianne, *Wicca: The Old Religion in the New Age*, Routledge & Kegan Paul, 1989

Eliade, Mircea, 'Some observations on European Witchcraft', in *Occultism, Witchcraft and Cultured Fashions*, University of Chicago Press, 1976

Farrar, Stewart, *What Witches Do*, Phoenix, 1983

Green, Marian, *A Witch Alone*, Aquarian, 1991

Hutton, Ronald, *The Pagan Religions of the Ancient British Isles*, Blackwell, 1991

Moorey, Teresa, *Witchcraft – a beginner's guide*, Hodder & Stoughton, 1996

Murray, Margaret, *The Witch Cult in Western Europe*, Oxford University Press, 1921

Shan, *Circlework – A DIY Handbook for Working Ritual, Psychology and Magic*, House of the Goddess, 1994

Starhawk, *The Spiral Dance*, Harper & Row, 1989

Valiente, Doreen, *An ABC of Witchcraft, Past & Present*, Hale, 1984

5
CYCLES AND
CELEBRATIONS

*To everything there is a season,
and a time to every purpose under Heaven*

Ecclesiastes 3:1

Most pagans mark the turning of the seasons in some way. They are a metaphor for our lives, from birth, through maturity into old age and death and they confirm our earthly state, for we are all soaked by the rain, swept by the wind and blossom in the sunshine. This thought can be humbling, but it is also uplifting, for it gives us a sense of something greater than us of which we are a part. Rituals, celebrations and folk customs are all designed to affirm this. Pagans who live in cities are all the more likely to seek this sense of connection, a relief from the alienated feeling of concrete and clay.

In my *Witchcraft – a beginner's guide*, I consider the meaning of the yearly cycle from the perspective of a solo witch. In the ancient 'mystery religions' such as that of Eleusis rites were secret, and that is still the case to some extent with Wicca today. However, there can be several levels of involvement in pagan culture. Folk customs and superstitions were – and are – the ways ordinary people had of marking the seasonal round. It is a way of accessing the spiritual nourishment of Nature. Honouring the seasons helps us to honour the processes of growth and change within ourselves, and this cyclicity has been respected since ancient times and carved in spiral symbols on stones and cave walls.

Here we shall look at some folk customs that are mainly British, although the true meaning of the times and seasons can only be discovered by inward journeys, and is quite incommunicable. It is worth noting that only the 'minor' mysteries of Eleusis were secret. The inner mystery, which is about union with the divine, was not secret. This is because it cannot be told – only experienced. The best way to approach this is first to get as much contact with the natural world as you can. This is so easily overlooked in quests for something arcane. Secondly, practise trance/visualisation. (See *Witchcraft – a beginner's guide*.)

The Wheel of the Year

The seasonal cycle is often depicted as a wheel with eight spokes or segments, for there are eight Sabbats or festivals in all, and the circle turns perpetually, one season leading to another, growth followed by maturity, decay and death, then producing new life again. Each part of the cycle is linked to a direction, an element, a stage in the evolution of the story of the Goddess and God, with other special gods and goddesses, and with totem animals. We can see the Goddess as the Wheel itself – the process of life – and the God as Son/Sun travelling around it. There is more than one version of the Wheel of the Year (sometimes called The Medicine Wheel) and this is explored at length by Kathy Jones in *Spinning the Wheel of Ana* (Ariadne, 1994). The best idea is to construct your own 'Wheel of the Year' and enter the feelings and associations that are important to you. As you begin to explore these ideas and attune yourself to the cycle you will find your understanding of the subject will deepen.

The cycle starts with Samhain (pronounced *sa-**ween***) On 31 October, which is also called Hallowe'en, and this is the Celtic New Year. The Goddess is present as Wise Crone, the God is Lord of the Underworld. Then at the Winter Solstice or Yule (22 Dec) the Goddess as Great Mother gives birth to the God anew, as the Divine Child. At Imbolc (2 Feb) we celebrate especially the inspiration of

Wheel of the Year

41

the Goddess as Maiden, but also as Mother, for She has recently given birth. At the Spring Equinox (21 March) both Goddess and God are youthful. The Maiden Goddess is bright with potential and in the greenwood the God grows to maturity. At Beltane (30 April) the Goddess and God mate and celebrate their sexuality. At Midsummer (22 June) the Goddess and God both glow with fulfilment of their union. The Goddess gives birth to nature, and again at harvest time, Lammas, (31 July) She gives birth to the grain and fruits. Then at the Autumn Equinox (21 Sept) again we celebrate the last of the harvest. The God is cut down with the corn at Lammas, and He is reborn, in a sense, in the loaves and produce made from the harvest. in another sense He begins a journey to the Underworld, to reign as Lord of Death at Samhain, and to be born again at Yule. This is all told from the perspective of the Northern Hemisphere, however. Many Australians prefer to 'rotate' the Wheel, marking Beltane at the start of November, Yule in the middle of the year, and so on.

Of course, this cycle is full of paradox and contradiction. The Goddess and God are within us always, but we focus on different aspects of them for a more vivid experience at different times. The God is seen as dying and reborn, but the Goddess is envisioned as changing Her face. In addition to the 'story' given above there is another aspect to the God cycle – that of the Holly King and Oak King. The Holly King is King of the Waning Year, as the Sun fades from Midsummer to Yule. He and the Oak King battle at Midsummer, and the Holly King wins. They battle again at Yule, and the Oak King is victorious. The Oak King rules the Waxing Year, from Yule to Midsummer. Holly and Oak represent the light and dark sides, but dark does not mean evil. It signifies things that are quiet, hidden, perhaps necessarily destructive, but containing wisdom. It is important to pagans to honour darkness as well as light, for that way is balanced, and not repressed.

Also, to understand the Goddess more fully we need to remember that She is Triple – Maiden, Mother and Crone, and each of these three aspects is equally valuable. Some pagans see the cycle in terms of the Goddess alone, some include the God, as Wiccans do. You can explore your own ideas of Goddess and God, and also the many personifications which we looked at briefly in Chapter 3. The Goddess can be Great Mother, She can be Triple Goddess, or She can appear in a hundred different ways as Venus, Freya, Morrigan or Brigit. Similarly the God can be young/old, light/dark or He can come in the guise of Herne the Hunter, Osiris or Odin. In short, it is what works for you that is important.

Samhain (31 October)

Mists creep in early, leaves fall, nights grow longer. This is an eerie time when the veil between us and the world of the spirits is thin. Ghosts – and witches – walk abroad, and we remember the Ancestors, both recent and from the distant past. The Christian festival of All Souls Day is on 2 November. 'Samhain' is usually taken to mean 'summer's end' but this is the start of a fresh cycle. We sweep up leaves, prune and cut – and plant bulbs to grow in the spring.

The best-known symbol of Hallowe'en is the pumpkin, hollowed out, with a candle shining through its grinning mask. This is the face of the Crone, She Who Watches. The native turnip lantern was also used to frighten away spirits by those who walked out into the night. Another meaning is that in the darkness light continues, hidden in tubers, seeds, dormant under the earth but still glowing, like the candle in the pumpkin. Besides this, Samhain is a time to think about masks – like the lantern face. We all wear them, showing faces to the world that are only an aspect of our true selves, and at this time of transformation we may like to change our mask/s or even dare to drop them altogether for a while. A mask is not just a disguise however – it can also be an invocation. Wearing the correct mask can call forth aspects of ourselves, from deep within. A similar idea can be the wearing of an animal skin – we can wear a bearskin to draw out the fierce 'bear' from inside us.

So the simple Hallowe'en lantern has lots of meanings, like most things. A pumpkin lantern is easy to make, for the inside is usually quite soft. Swedes and turnips are more traditionally British, but they are harder to hollow and carve. Cut a piece out of the top of the pumpkin, with the stalk at the centre. Make sure this is reasonably large, for you'll need to be able to get your hand down it. Then you can scoop out the seeds with your hands and hollow the inside out with a fairly sharp spoon. Some pumpkins require a fair bit of hollowing to be thin enough to cut the face; others hardly need any at all, but you will probably want to remove the threads the seeds were attached to. Draw a face on the outside (you can buy kits for this) and cut through with a small, sharp knife. If the eyes, nose and mouth are big enough there will be enough oxygen to keep the candle alight when the 'hat' is put back on. Put the pumpkin, complete with candle inside in your window and wait for the Trick or Treaters.

Trick or Treat seems to have arisen in the United States – but it is a revival of older, similar customs from Europe. Children dressed as vampires and ghouls knock at doors demanding a 'treat' and if one is not forthcoming – beware!

This has been criticised for a variety of reasons, but basically it seems very healthy. Boundaries are down now, and the spirit of the season is honoured by the 'trickers'. We are not all sweetness and light and neither is nature. It is better to acknowledge this symbolically by a bit of harmless fun than to deny it.

For the Celts, Samhain was the start of the story-telling season. In our family we mark this by telling ghost/horror stories by candlelight. Each person holds the fort for a specified time, usually two minutes, as any longer can be hard for children. When time is up the next person takes over, and it is interesting how the emphasis of the story shifts, from the gothic graveyards-and-white-sheets of the youngsters, through macabre teenage humour to a more subtle adult approach. The atmosphere is lifted by someone's funny ending, lights go on and it's supper-time.

Apple-bobbing is a favourite game at Hallowe'en parties. Although ruled by Venus the apple is associated with the Crone and with Underworld knowledge and wisdom. Cut an apple crossways and you will see a star shape at the centre – the five-point star shape is sacred to the Goddess. The apple must be pulled out of the water with your teeth. The animal instinct is foremost, human hands must not be used, and if you end up with your head under water that could mean the waters of the unconscious overwhelming a mind that has become too sophisticated. A little beer or cider will help!

The major festivals of Samhain, Imbolc, Beltane and Lammas are believed to be older in origin, arising from herding cultures, whereas the later agrarian people became more concerned with the exact position of the sun at the equinoxes and solstices. These were fire festivals and sometimes human sacrifice may have been practised. Often it would have been the king who willingly died, as the God 'dies'. It has been said that human sacrifice was a later, patriarchal innovation and that the older matrifocal societies did not practise it. No one can be sure. Nowadays it is a horrifying thought, but it's interesting that in Britain we have our bonfires on 5 November to burn not a king, but the would-be king-slayer, Guy Fawkes.

The purpose of Samhain ritual is to create an atmosphere where the spirit world feels close enough to be tangible. Also we wish to honour the forces of death, for it is death that gives life its purpose and decay that fertilises new growth. Sex, added to birth and death, forms a trio of transformation. Fertility is honoured at Samhain in the nuts and fruits we may gather, but there is a side to sexuality that has little to do with procreation and far more to do with the experience sexual passion can give us of darker parts of our personality, its role in deep transformation and connection with spirituality and karma. This is also remembered. The Sun is now in Scorpio, water sign of passion and transformation. The element of water is connected with feeling and remembering, and Scorpio is ruled by Pluto, dark lord of the Underworld.

Yule (22 December)

This is the depth of winter, and some traditions interpret this as a time of death, but it is also birth, for at this point the Sun begins to make the return journey. All of our well-known Christmas customs celebrate the return of light in some way, the power of the birth-giving Goddess and the advent of the Magical Child, the Sun/Son God. Many religions mark the birth of a divine child, at some point.

Winter solstice

If we look behind the dogmas and outer trappings in truth we all worship the same god/dess. At Yule the brotherhood of man is remembered in the Christmas spirit and the message of love and new birth.

At Christmas, which comes three days after Yule, we exchange presents. These are our gifts for the Divine Child, as all new babies are showered with gifts. It is often said that Christmas is a 'time for children', and especially it is a time for the child of the Goddess, the bright Sun that now begins to grow in strength.

Father Christmas is a well-known figure. He is reminiscent of the witches' Horned God, Herne/Cernunnos, with his horned reindeer. Also his hearty laugh and rosy cheeks suggest the Oak King, whose reign now begins again. The merry Horned God was debased as the Christian Devil, who is also called 'Old Nick', and Father Christmas is also called Saint Nicholas, or Saint Nick. He may also have developed from the German goddess Holda, who dressed in red and came down the chimney with gifts.

Evergreen trees are sacred to the Goddess, for they retain their greenery all year round, as opposed to deciduous trees, whose leaves die. Almost everyone has a Christmas tree, decorated with brilliant baubles that catch the light and seem to conjure the return of the Sun. On the top of the tree we place our Christmas Fairy – yet another Goddess image, to honour the birth-giving Mother. We also decorate our homes with holly (for the departing Holly King) and mistletoe. Some say mistletoe is sacred to the Sun, but I prefer the Moon as ruler, for the berries are moon-white and their juice is like semen, which is ruled by the Moon. Whichever you prefer, the seventeenth-century herbalist Culpeper says that mistletoe is best grown on the oak – so mistletoe is for the Oak King. We kiss underneath it for fertility and happiness.

Other winter customs are Mumming Plays and pantomimes: merry slapsticks that celebrate the seasonal spirit. Wassailing – a noisy ceremony to drive away harm from apple trees – is a local tradition in apple-growing English counties. The Roman Saturnalia took place at this season, and was a time of role-reversal and generally 'letting it all hang out'. The Sun enters Capricorn, Earth sign of the goat. The goat is a great climber, and the Sun now climbs in the sky. Capricorn is ruled by Saturn: although known for discipline, there is another side to Capricorn that is lusty, well-deserving of the goat's horns and quite at home in the wildness of Saturnalia.

In Wiccan covens, two male coven members are usually chosen to act as Holly King and Oak King, and they enact a symbolic struggle, which is won by the Oak King, of course. The ritual emphasises the return and rebirth of the Sun and of the God.

IMBOLC (2 FEBRUARY)

Days are lengthening and although the weather may be cold we are aware that life is definitely stirring. White snowdrops dance in the sharp wind and ewe's milk flows with the birth of the lambs. The Sun is now in the sign of the Water-Bearer, Aquarius, which is an air sign bringing the waters of en-light-enment at this festival of Light.

At Imbolc the accent is on the Goddess, both as Mother (She gave birth to the Sun God about six weeks ago, and all mothers will be familiar with the 'six weeks check-up') and as inspirational Maid. Imbolc is the Feast of the Poets, when we celebrate the flame of creativity. The goddess Brigit is especially honoured at this time: originally she was a form of the Triple Goddess. One of the customs associated with Imbolc is the making of a Bridie Doll by dressing up a sheaf of oats in women's clothing and later placing it in the earth. This has links with fertility rites. The women of Glastonbury in Somerset have developed this beautifully:

> *Instead of being placed in the earth the Bridie Dolls live on.*
> *The new Bridie is introduced to the previous years' Bridie*
> *Dolls in a ceremony at the sacred well. She joins the circle of*
> *the Mothers and Grandmothers of the previous years,*
> *although the new Bridie's particular energy governs the*
> *coming year. Thus the accumulating wisdom of the*
> *Ancestors is honoured through the years.*

(Kathy Jones, *Spinning the Wheel of Ana*, Ariadne, 1994)

Shan, Priestess of the House of the Goddess (see 'Resources') tells us of their lovely custom associated with the Bridie Doll. She travels around to different houses and then returns to base to be put in a sacred Bed. Each woman then takes it in turns to share her Bed and to tell of feelings and experiences about motherhood and birth – youngest first. Meanwhile the men toast the Goddess at the pub and are given a right royal welcome when they return for the final feast. A woman could do this on her own, with her own special Bridie doll, dreaming or meditating about mothering and anything related, and perhaps writing down thoughts or poetry if she wishes. Make your own Bridie Doll if you like – it doesn't matter how amateurish you feel your efforts are. This is a good time for men to renew commitment to the Goddess.

The Roman Feast of Lupercalia, which took place on 15 February, was sacred to Pan. It was a time of unruly fertility ceremony and cleansing. St Valentine's day (14 February) is when couples declare their love – 'coming clean' and hoping for fulfilment. 'Lupercalia' derives partly from *lupus* – Latin for wolf. Sacred to Brigit are the wild wolf, wise snake, the fertile cow and the far-sighted bird of prey. You may like to consider these creatures and what they mean for us at this time of awakening, and to think of new beginnings and creative projects.

Rituals at this time are about the re-emergence of life and a celebration of the Triple Goddess.

Spring Equinox (21 March)

The Sun now enters the fire sign Aries, sign of the impetuous Ram. Light and dark are in balance but light is gaining. Life is now establishing itself in the spring flowers and longer days. Easter, named after the goddess Eostre, the Teutonic Maid goddess of the earth, is calculated by the Moon, occurring on the first Sunday after the first Full Moon after the Equinox. We are familiar with Easter's Christian theme of sacrificial death and resurrection, and this echoes similar pagan traditions of sacrificial gods that die and resurrect like the Sun does yearly. In our spring-cleaning we make way for the new, and it is a good idea also to do this inwardly.

Hot cross buns are traditional Good Friday fare. The cross has many meanings and this equal-armed Celtic cross means the four elements or directions, the four seasons and is really a Wheel of the Year itself.

The hare links several strands of myth. Sacred to the Moon Goddess, witches were thought to shape-shift into hares. The hare

49

has been known as a self-sacrificing animal, so maybe connected with the sacrificial god. Rabbits acquire some of the hare's mystery. The Easter Bunny is a symbol of fertility, said to bring the Easter eggs, and eggs of course are a metaphor for the life that is 'hatching' everywhere now.

When I was small it was the 'bells', not the Easter bunny, who brought the Easter eggs. In this European tradition, the bells returned to Rome after their silence during Lent, dropping eggs on their way. Bells are also a much older symbol. Their round shape makes them special to the Goddess and their ringing often marks significant points in rituals.

Eggs can be decorated for friends and family at this time. Use food colouring, and plenty of imagination.

The wheel is an important symbol for Wiccans at this festival, meaning the circle of the seasons in perfect balance (also echoing the Hot Cross Buns). The theme of the festival is the Sun's growth in power.

Beltane (30 April)

This has been called the oldest and most important festival, for nature is riotous and blooming and everyone feels the stirrings of vitality and sexuality. The Sun is in Taurus, an earth sign ruled by Venus and known for its sensuality. The best-known symbol of Beltane is the maypole – a phallic pole planted deep in the receptive earth. To wash your face in the early morning dew of May Day was believed to guarantee continuing youth and beauty.

As people danced around the maypole, holding the ribbons that trailed from the top, the winding and unwinding of the spiral of life was enacted. Dowsers (see Chapter 2) can sometimes detect patterns of energy where the dancers trod. One of the tallest maypoles now standing is in the village of Paganhill – appropriately named – near Stroud in Gloucestershire. It is painted red, white and blue – very patriotic colours, but they are also the colours of the Triple Goddess. White is for the Maiden, red for the Mother and blue (though more usually black) for the Crone. This is yet another example of hidden pagan meanings. The Puritans were alive to the sexual symbolism of the maypole and it was banned, but Charles II reintroduced it during the Restoration.

The custom of going 'A-Maying' meant staying out all night to gather hawthorn, watching the sun rise and no doubt making love in the greenwood – the so-called 'greenwood marriage'. Mark this festival by gathering hawthorn yourself if you wish. There are many merry customs all over Europe to celebrate this time, with dancing, flowers, music and processions. In many places a young girl is crowned as May Queen, and this has links with Maid Marion of English folk legend. Maid Marion is really the Maiden herself, greenwood goddess of the deer, the hare, the secret and the fertile places of the forest. Her consort Robin Hood is also the Green Man, or Pan – the spirit of lawless nature himself.

The cross-quarter festivals were all celebrated by bonfires. Cattle were driven between two fires at Beltane for luck and a good milk yield. As with other festivals the indoor substitute for the Bel-fire is a candle in the cauldron. Beltane is named after the Celtic god Bel, the 'bright one'.

Rituals now emphasise sexual allure and the joy of healthy sensuality. Celebrate with a party, excursion or barbecue – whatever feels right for you.

Midsummer (22 June)

The Sun is at the height of his powers, although June is not the warmest month in Britain. Now we celebrate the very peak of summer and the things we have brought to fruition, remembering that as this point is reached, so begins the inevitable journey back into darkness. As everything in the world of vegetation seems to be coming to full fruition the Sun enters the nurturing water sign of Cancer. A woman who wishes to conceive should walk naked through her vegetable garden on Midsummer's Eve, preferably picking some St John's Wort. This is a solar herb that flowers at this time. Among other things it is

Summer solstice

said to be effective against melancholy and madness – so explain that to the neighbours if they spot you!

The great stone circle of Stonehenge is now subject to restricted entry. There are probably many reasons for the construction of this majestic temple of stone and winds, the Giant's Dance. On Midsummer's Day the Sun rises directly over the Hele Stone. The ancients probably were more deeply attuned to the rhythms of land and sky and the penetrating solar rays represented the divine meeting of Earth and Sun. This is the Druid feast of Alban Heruin, 'The Light of the Shore', their most complex ceremony, preceded by an all night vigil round the solstice fire. The following Dawn Ceremony used to be performed at Stonehenge before it was banned – rather like banning the Pope from the Vatican! You may like to have your own dawn vigil, going to a special high place and watching the Sun come up, if the weather is clear.

On a lighter note, this is the time of year for Morris Dances in Britain. The Morris Men (or 'Mary's Men'?) dance in honour of the Goddess, waving the white handkerchiefs of the Maid, their bells, ribbons and ribaldry strongly suggesting fertility rites – a repeating theme. In the United States, 4 July is Independence Day – a significant time to proclaim liberty. Shan reminds us that this is a time of large gatherings, so go to a pop concert, cricket match or even Wimbledon.

Rituals emphasise the power of the Sun and the glory of summer flowers. This is a festival of water as well as fire, which were both seen by the ancients as transformative. The Sun is now in the water sign of Cancer, setting sail for the south. The drama of the Holly King and the Oak King are enacted in some way by Wiccans, with Holly winning this time, as the year begins to wane.

Lughnasadh (31 July)

This means 'Feast of Lugh' and is pronounced **Loo**-*nus-ah*. Lugh was god of fire and light to the Celts. Another perhaps more usual name for this festival is Lammas, meaning 'loaf-mass'.

Now the air is heavy with fruitfulness and the Sun seems to have come to earth. Lammas/Lughnasadh takes place between the hay and grain harvests, but really it marks the start of the harvesting proper for most produce is gathered in between now and the Autumn Equinox. It is a time to think of the harvests in our own lives, too.

A phenomenon often seen especially in the Wiltshire fields is the crop circle – stalks bent in perfect circular shapes, that are often quite complex. Some of these may be hoaxes, but whether this is the case or not, or whether some mysterious earth-energy or even extra-terrestrials are responsible, these circles are a reminder of the spiral of life and the relationship of crops to ancient powers of Sun and soil. Some people try sleeping in the centre of these circles and the resulting dreams are sometimes vivid and meaningful.

Perhaps the best-known seasonal custom at this time is the making of the Corn Dolly. The best ears from the last sheaf cut would be taken and made into a corn dolly, which was generally kept over the hearth for good fortune. The seeds were then shaken out and sown with the new seeds the following spring. The traditional colour for tying or dressing the Corn Dolly is red – colour of life and the Earth Mother. You can make your own simple Corn Dolly from a few ears of wheat, but just take a few from the edge of the field out of respect for the farmer.

This is a festival of life, in the harvest, but also loss, for the Corn Spirit is cut down, and the Sun begins to 'die'. Please note, the British meaning of 'corn' is usually wheat, and nothing like the corn-on-the-cob that may be more familiar in the States.

The focus of ritual now is to celebrate the harvest and to mark the death – and life – of the God. We mark the positive aspects of sacrifice. Now is a good time to make a pledge to do something specific for the earth – perhaps planting a tree.

Αυτυmn Εquinοχ (21 Septεmbεr)

As at the Spring Equinox light and dark are in balance, but now dark is gaining, The last of the harvests have now been gathered and thanks can be said for the successful completion. The Sun enters Libra, air sign of balance and peace. There is a sense of shifting gear as life prepares to retreat and we think about what we must put to one side as winter advances.

This was the time of the Eleusinian Mysteries, about which we know little for the initiates kept the secrets closely guarded. However, it seems that some of the rituals centred upon the descent of

Persephone/Kore to the Underworld, to reign as Queen until summer. This is not hard to interpret: only by going within and facing darkness, both in ourselves and the coming winter, are we able to obey the Eleusinian instruction, 'Know thyself'.

The obvious custom is making preserves, jams and chutneys from the seasonal produce which I have always done 'religiously'. Now in Britain it is time to gather blackberries from the hedgerows. There is nothing like the satisfaction of making blackberry pie from your very own 'harvest': you may like to have your own 'harvest supper' to give thanks for the bounty of the earth.

Wiccan rituals centre upon a single ear of wheat, which echoes the climax (it is said) of the Eleusinian ritual where the initiate was shown an ear of wheat and told, 'In silence is the seed of wisdom gained'.

Moon observance

The rhythms of the Moon are at least as important as those of the Sun. While the Sun is linked to consciousness and reasoning the Moon is associated with the unconscious, and regarded as 'feminine'. Instinct and femininity are close to the hearts of the pagans generally. Earth is the body of the Goddess, but the gleaming Moon, waxing as Maiden, Full as Mother and waning as Crone is Her celestial manifestation. The Moon rules menstruation and the tides of life. Her phases affect the growth of plants, the incidence of accidents, bleeding from wounds, and entry to mental hospitals. She also rules the entry into the Mysteries of self-knowledge, body-knowledge and spiritual experiences.

As mistress of magic and starlight vision, the Moon is very important to solo witches who may choose to mark her phases with a variety of rituals and activities. Wiccan non-festival meetings are called Esbats and these are traditionally held at Full Moon. A beautiful Wiccan ceremony is that of 'Drawing Down the Moon' – also done as part of the opening ritual to Sabbats. Here the Moon Goddess is invoked upon the High Priestess, who recites *The Charge*, the words of which are lovely and have been largely re-styled by Doreen

Charge of the Goddess

Valiente, from older material. This is probably the best 'statement' of Goddess-worship available, so it is quoted here in all its full beauty:

Whenever ye have need of anything, once in the month, better it be when the Moon is full, then shall ye gather together in some secret place and adore the spirit of me who am Queen of all witches. There shall ye assemble, ye who would fain learn all sorcery, yet have not yet won its deepest secrets. To thee will I teach things as yet unknown. And ye shall be free from slavery, and as a sign that ye be truly free ye shall be naked in your rites; and ye shall dance, sing, feast, make music and love all in my praise, for mine is the ecstasy of the spirit and mine also is joy on earth, for my law is love unto all things. Keep pure your highest ideal, strive ever towards it, let naught stop you or turn you aside. For mine is the secret door that opens upon the Land of Youth, and mine is the cup of the wine of Life, and the Cauldron of Cerridwen, which is the Holy Grail of immortality. I am the gracious Goddess who gives the gift of joy unto the heart of man. Upon earth I give knowledge of the spirit eternal. Beyond death I give peace, freedom and reunion with those who have gone before. Nor do I demand sacrifice, for behold, I am the Mother of all living, and my love is poured out upon the earth.

[Here the high priest says: 'Hear ye the words of the Star Goddess. She in the dust of whose feet are the hosts of Heaven, whose body encircles the Universe.']

I, who am the beauty of the green earth and the white moon among the stars and the mystery of the waters and the desire of the heart of man, call unto thy soul. Arise and come unto me for I am the soul of Nature who gives life to the Universe. From me all things proceed, and to me all things must return, and before my face, beloved of gods and men, let thine innermost divine self be enfolded in the rapture of the Infinite. Let my worship be within the heart that rejoiceth; for behold, all acts of love and pleasure are my rituals. And therefore let there be beauty and strength,

*power and compassion, honour and humility, mirth and
reverence within you. And thou who thinkest to seek for me,
know thy searching and yearning shall avail thee not unless
thou knowest the mystery; that if that which thou seekest
thou findest not within thee thou wilt never find it without
thee. For behold I have been with thee from the beginning
and I am that which is attained at the end of desire.*

Lunar rhythms are important to our lives and often neglected. You
may like to make them a part of your life by simply noting the day
of Full Moon and buying a bottle of wine to toast our Mother in her
glory. Try lighting a candle – perhaps a red one, for that is the colour
associated with the Mother, but any colour you like will do – to
mark this special time. Full Moon is a good time to meditate on our
wild and instinctual side. To find out more about the phases of the
Moon and their connection with the Goddess you may like to read
The Moon and You in this series.

pRACTICE

This chapter has given you many seasonal things to do. Begin by
thinking about the next festival to come and listing all the things
about it that come to your mind, both personal and general.

Make your own 'Wheel of the Year'. Don't be afraid to enter your
own associations, even if you don't know what they mean –
meanings may become clearer at a later date.

With the Moon, begin by noting her phases in your diary, taking
moonlit walks and noticing how your energy grows, reduces, is
applied in different ways, and how your emotions fluctuate with the
phases.

Further information

Farrar, Janet and Stewart, *Eight Sabbats for Witches*, Hale, 1981

Green, Marian, *A Calendar of Festivals*, Element, 1991

Howard, Michael, *The Sacred Ring*, Capall Bann

Moorey, Teresa, *The Moon and You for Beginners*, Hodder & Stoughton, 1996

Stepanich, Kisma K., *The Gaia Tradition*, Llewellyn, 1991

CHAPTER

6

SCI-FI, PSYCHOLOGY AND THE FOUR ELEMENTS

... it was not possible to express as separate ideas in the Martian tongue the human concepts: 'religion', 'philosophy' and 'science' ... All such ... were simply 'learnings' which came from the 'Old Ones'.

Robert Heinlein, *Stranger in a Strange Land*

We know that pagans are inspired by myths drawn from ancient times. However, some are also fired by personalities and ideas from science fiction. This is not as surprising as it may seem, for ancient gods and aliens can both be termed 'archetypal', meaning they embody principles from the Collective Unconscious. This is a deep fund of universal experience that we all share, that we sometimes enter in dreams, that we may be overwhelmed by in psychosis, and that we draw upon in states of trance and magical work. Inspired authors such as the best science fiction writers have a type of 'hotline' to this well of symbolism and are able to bring things to life for us, as are the myths of Persephone, Pan, Cerridwen, and other gods. In addition many science fiction works have a prophetic tinge. For instance, George Orwell's *1984* is to some extent with us now, for Big Brother watches us more than we realise, with our names and intimate personal records stored in computers we know not where.

The psychologist C. G. Jung taught that myth was important, for mythic dramas are an allegory of what goes on in the personality. Contemplating myths is fascinating even when we don't analyse them for their relevance. They can also draw us nearer to a feeling of wholeness, which brings us closer to the divine – so really in using myths we are looking inwards, and around. The image that this gives rise to is the circle, and we shall be looking at this further. Sci-fi is modern myth. Although it lacks the dignity of antiquity it can be as evocative as the most ancient stories.

One of the most inspiring novels seems to have been Robert Heinlein's *Stranger in a Strange Land* which was popular in the Sixties. It tells of an earth boy raised on Mars by aliens. When he returns to Earth he is bewildered, finding it hard to understand things that most humans regard as basic, but with a deep respect for life. The main purpose of a Martian's life is to experience fully the entirety of things – a mystical union that is sought by many pagans. In water-brotherhood, one of the principal ceremonies, water is shared and a deep bond formed. Water is the basis of all life and widely symbolic. Water rituals, such as hand-washing, sometimes arise spontaneously in groups. Heinlein's novel still inspires the Church of All Worlds, a pagan organisation founded in the 1960s in America and still going strong, with branches in Australia. One of their exhortations is 'Never thirst'. Spiritual thirst can be slacked by participation in nature, so Heinlein's novel is an account of what we seek today.

Another well-known science fiction saga is that of *Star Trek*, still alive and well in various forms after 30 years. Their mission 'To boldly go where no man has gone before' is a brave statement about the spirit of humanity. The message of respect and co-operation between nations and alien species is also attractive. *Star Trek* has a large cult following, with trekkies dressing up as their favourite characters. Of course, this seems far from religion in the more accepted sense, but as we have seen, paganism is about quests, not dogma, and *Star Trek* is a quest *par excellence* 'to seek out new worlds and new civilisations'. It is the original *Star Trek* that is interesting for our purpose here, in the shape of the four main characters, Captain Kirk, Mr Spock, Dr 'Bones' McCoy and Scottie, with his engines.

To understand the importance of these four we need to return to Jung again and look at his concept of the Four Functions of Consciousness. Jung was a pioneering intellect. He made connections between ancient wisdom – practices such as alchemy – and modern analytical psychology in a way that has enabled us to build bridges between ancient and modern and value what might otherwise be dismissed as primitive or superstitious. The idea of the Four Elements (Air, Water, Fire and Earth) and their link with personality is embedded in many cultures. It corresponds with the twelve astrological signs, which divide into groups of three under each element. These are Fire (Aries, Leo, Sagittarius), Earth (Taurus, Virgo, Capricorn), Air (Gemini, Libra, Aquarius) and Water (Cancer, Scorpio, Pisces). Jung developed this idea into four basic functions of consciousness – Thinking (Air), Feeling (Water), Intuition (Fire) and Sensation (Earth).

According to Jung each individual has one or two of these functions dominant, while the others are mostly unconscious. Thinking and feeling Jung described as 'evaluative'. Feeling in this sense does not mean strong emotion. It means evaluating in terms of humanity, family, nearest and dearest; whereas thinking also evaluates, but by means of logic. Thinking and feeling are polar opposites and it is hard for both to be conscious at once. A person whose dominant function is feeling will find it hard to use logic to any great extent and will certainly not make any major decisions on the basis of it. A feeling person is likely to be in tune with current mores of the society s/he lives in and to be conscious of the reactions and feelings of other people. When called upon to say what s/he thinks s/he will still say what s/he feels, because it will be hard to identify 'thinking'. Thinking will thus be an 'inferior' function. This doesn't mean s/he doesn't think, but it may emerge as half-baked second-hand ideas and some surprisingly rigid and prejudiced opinions which s/he may adhere to stubbornly.

Someone whose thinking is the superior function values logic and believes people should say what they mean. Truth and reason are all-important and emotions are suspect. However, this doesn't mean the 'thinking' type doesn't have feelings – s/he does – and because these are relegated to the unconscious they are often very primitive and may take the ascetic intellectual one day by storm. The sort of scenario that may illustrate this is the professor who falls desperately in love with the prostitute. The thinking type also finds himself ambushed by inconvenient emotions in smaller ways, and may exude an inky atmosphere of jealousy, which he will strenuously deny but which everyone is aware of. Despite the labels, none of the functions has the monopoly on intelligence, for all are able to use memory and meaningful association of ideas, but in different ways.

Intuition and sensation are another pair of opposites, and these functions Jung called 'perceptual' because they concern ways of perceiving existence, rather than evaluating. Sensation function is the reality function, for the sensation type is rooted in the here and now and the evidence of his five senses. Sensation types often appear very sensible, but they are not necessarily logical. Intuitives, on the other hand, inhabit the world of possibilities. They are people with hunches, projecting their consciousness into the future or the past, sowing many seeds of inspiration, but rarely staying to reap. What they perceive is other realms – things that can't be put into words. But that doesn't mean they are necessarily airy-fairy or ineffectual. If they have the courage of their convictions they are very dynamic, and may be directors of successful companies or players on the stockmarket.

The four functions

The diagram (overleaf) shows consciousness as a circle divided into the four segments of thinking, feeling, intuition and sensation, and it is possible to see from this that if your main function is feeling you may have access to sensation and intuition on either side, but your thinking will be the most inaccessible. Similarly, if you are an intuitive, feeling and thinking may be possible but the sensation function will be the most difficult. Some people have two functions well developed and these are likely to be side-by-side, such as feeling and intuition. By middle age people often have access to three functions. It is the integration of the fourth function into consciousness that may be most elusive and is one of the goals of self-development.

The idea of the four elements/functions can be called 'archetypal' and so holds unending fascination. It turns up in astrology as Fire, Earth, Air and Water, and shows in figures of gods and goddesses, many of whom embody a particular element. Lugh, for example, is a fire god, connected to dying and resurrecting as flames do, as the Sun does, as the inspiration of intuitive people comes and goes. The entire idea has been very aptly embodied on TV screens in *Star Trek*.

I am sure by now you can tell which of the Starship *Enterprise* crew represents which function, but if you haven't done so yet, and if this whole concept is new to you, give a thought to which of the characters you associate with thinking, feeling, intuition and sensation before going on to the next paragraph.

The most obvious has to be Spock as the Thinker – ever logical and controlled. And with whom is he always arguing? With the Feeling Doctor, of course, who values human life and relationships. Kirk is the Intuitive captain, making split-second decisions on the basis of his hunches, and Scottie, with his engines, is the Sensation type, keeping the practicalities running smoothly.

This may all sound like a game, but it is far from that. Inexorably we are fascinated by our opposite. Thinking types are drawn to Feeling people, Intuitives to Sensation function, and thereby often hangs a tale of misery, frustration, incomprehension and heartache. It can be like living with an alien, and it can be so hard to realise that this person really does see the world totally differently, is both scared by and attracted to what you represent and really can't help it. And the same is true of you.

Thinking and Feeling types can have a difficult time. Thinker can't understand why Feeler is so illogical and uncontrolled – yet he longs to bask in that warmth of feeling. And Feeler can't understand why Thinker is so cold and unsympathetic – yet she longs for some of that detachment. Intuition and Sensation, being perceptual rather than evaluative don't have such a hard time, for they are more prone to let the other get on with it, walking hand in hand and parallel.

To determine which is your uppermost function it is sometimes easiest to consider what you can't do. Can't work keys, tools, objects, bewildered by car and kitchen – then you may be an Intuitive. Can't bear displays of emotion, want everything to be clear-cut and organised – then you are probably a Thinker. Can't see the point of logic, it's cold, a dead-end and you feel misunderstood – then perhaps you're a Feeling type. Feel mystified and suspicious about magic and the non-rational, and impatient with 'airy-fairy' people – then you may be a Sensation type. Your astrological sign is a good indication too. If you're a fire sign (Aries, Leo, Sagittarius) you may be an Intuitive; if earth (Taurus, Virgo, Capricorn), you may be a Sensation type; if air (Gemini, Libra, Aquarius), you may be a Thinker; and if water (Cancer, Scorpio, Pisces), you may be a Feeling type. However, it is far better to have your entire chart drawn up, to see where all the planets are.

You may have noticed that I've used 'he' mainly for Thinking and 'she' for Feeling, because that seems to be more often than not the way it is, but certainly it is not always so. Also you may notice that Thinking and Sensation have been valued by our culture, which is materialistic and scientifically logical, whereas the other functions are regarded with suspicion, or worse. Thus Intuitive and Feeling people may be more likely than others to try to develop other sides to themselves, to gain acceptance. However, paganism is about balance. The purpose of finding our inferior function is so we can develop it and understand better. Often the way to the divine is connected to the inferior function, and represented in fairy-tales and stories by a helpful animal or seemingly foolish or damaged person who leads the way to the 'happy ever after'. If you are fascinated by things that belong to your 'inferior' side, so much better, for there lies true knowledge and magic.

This brings us full circle, so to speak, back to the magic circle used in rites by magicians, witches, Wiccans and many pagans following similar paths. This is a circle that is created on the spirit plane by visualisation and anchored by ritual, and it is used for magical work and for the rites at Sabbats and Esbats. The purpose of this circle is for protection, for when we move into 'ritual consciousness' we are more open to stray energies. It is also for containment. Power raised can be kept within the circle until the moment of release. Creating the circle is also an important starting-point that tells our unconscious 'Here we go; let's get down to it'. It is also a symbol of wholeness and balance and a philosophical base.

The quartered circle, used in magic and ritual

An important part of creating the circle is the summoning of the Guardians, or Watchtowers as they as called by Wiccans. These are the protective and empowering spirits of the Elements and are invoked – inwardly called up – at each of the compass points, north, east, south and west, clockwise in that order. North corresponds to earth, east to air, south to fire and west to water. They are invoked by tracing a pentagram (five-pointed star) in the air, saying the appropriate words and visualising. North/earth corresponds to sensation, east/air to Thinking, south/fire to Intuition and west/water to Feeling. For north you may think of deep caves, soil and rich fields; for east clear air on a mountaintop, fresh breeze and light; for south imagine leaping flames, wild dances and hot sunshine; and for the west think of cool, green waters, fountains, the swell of the ocean. As you may guess, the function you find most difficult will probably be the Watchtower you struggle most to visualise and invoke when you begin to learn the ritual.

Entry into the ancient mystery cult of Eleusis involved the injunction 'Know thyself'. That is not easy, but it is something that many pagans are concerned with, at least to some degree. Paganism is hardly about self-analysis, although many pagans are healers, counsellors or psychotherapists of some sort. Covens and hearths are not encounter groups. However, paganism is about self-realisation and spiritual development, and wholeness is part of this process. Thinking about our superior and inferior functions can be a great help in understanding life in general and acquiring inner balance. The symbol of balance and wholeness, of the true self, is a mandala, which is a circular pattern. We are back to the circle again. Indeed the diagram of the Functions is a simple mandala.

The Wheel of the Year, the Medicine Wheel, the magic circle, the Four Functions, these are all mandalas. They are all ideas to turn around in your head, in your dreams, to play with, to be inspired by. Myths and stories turn the wheels, dramatise different parts of them and bring things to life. Pagans seeking a fuller experience of themselves and of nature, and wishing to explore, find inspiration and discover that true sense of self that finds the Self everywhere, may like to bear this in mind.

Jung put forward many ideas relevant to anyone on an esoteric path. For instance, his concept of the Shadow is very important. The Shadow is composed of the parts of us that are not conscious. It is the Dweller on the Threshold and it is one of the first things you meet when becoming involved in magic and trance. It is important to identify the Shadow as far as possible, for you won't be able to keep it out of your magic circle however much you sweep and banish. If you are sure you have 'risen above' it think again, because you may be deluding yourself. Contrary to popular belief, the shadow may contain desirable as well as undesirable things. It may hold power and talent – things we have kept at bay to make ourselves more acceptable. Starhawk, in her chapter on Trance in *The Spiral Dance* (Harper & Row, 1989) has valuable things to say on this subject.

Jung also tells us about the animus and anima: the 'inner man' for women and the 'inner woman' for men, respectively. Offering feminine ideas of the divine as well as masculine, paganism explores ways of understanding and relating to these parts of ourselves. None of these concepts are rigid, for they are being developed and explored by modern Jungians.

PRACTICE

What do you think are your superior and inferior functions? How do they manifest in your life and relationships? Are you attracted to types that are opposite to you? How have you experienced this? What can you do to make things easier for everyone concerned? Are you interested in developing your unconscious areas? How may exploration of your opposite make you feel more complete and connected? What myths, stories or science fiction fascinate you? And why do you think this is?

To find out what your Shadow self may be, write down all the things that you dislike or are irritated by in others. Look at the list and then sternly ask yourself where they apply to you. The chances are that they represent your Shadow. (I recommend doing this in the toilet and flushing the paper down the loo afterwards – but you won't forget what was on it!)

Further information

Bleakley, Alan, *Fruits of the Moon Tree*, Gateway, 1984

––––– *Earth's Embrace*, Gateway, 1989

Crowley, Vivianne, *Wicca: the Old Religion in the New Age*, Aquarian, 1989

Fordham, Frieda, *An Introduction to Jung's Psychology*, Pelican, 1985

von Franz, M.-L., Jung, C. G., *et al.*, *Man and His Symbols*, Pan/Picador, 1978

Greene, Liz, *Astrology for Lovers*, Unwin, 1986

—— *Relating*, Aquarian, 1986

Jung, C. G. , *Memories, Dreams and Reflections*, Flamingo/Fontana, 1983

—— *Analytical Psychology*, Ark/Routledge & Kegan Paul, 1986

Pratchett, Terry, *The Colour of Magic* (a novel), Corgi, 1993

7 shamanism

Worlds spin fast when I stamp my feet
Body moves to an ancient beat
I will dance 'til my spirit bleeds ...
Shaman-Ca, Shaman-Ca, Shaman-Ca

Carolyn Hillyer 'Shaman-Ca' from the album
Grandmother Turtle, Seventh Wave Music, 1994

A shamanic experience

Our image of the capering medicine man is very far from New-Agers seeking enlightenment in jeans and sequined waistcoats, and yet shamanism is becoming more and more popular today among those wishing for contact with the transcendent. Before we look at what shamanism is and what its relevance may be for us in the present day, let us start with an actual experience.

This is an encounter of my own. While I've done a fair bit of trance-work, there can always be a deeper experience. I wondered what it was, if anything that made 'shamanism' different. To me the answer turned out to be quite simple – the difference is in the drumbeat.

About thirty of us, all interested in subjects that can be called esoteric, gathered together to hear a talk on shamanism, and find out for ourselves. We are grouped in a circle, two deep. In the centre our guides for the evening had set out a Medicine Wheel, based on symbolism from the Lakota tradition. (There are about 400 different tribes in North America, all with their own variations on the Wheel and its symbols.) 'Medicine' means power, and the power symbols were placed at the four compass points, arranged on a circular mat. This is very similar to the witches' circle although there is a difference in the association between elements and quarters – and this circle was simply an image to conjure with, or so it seemed. All the protection, all the power conveyed by a witches' circle was to be given and controlled by the drum.

The circle represents the cycle of life. The east is the place of morning, of spirit, fire and spring. It is a doorway, a seed-place, a pre-embryonic stage. In the east of the circle were grouped yellow stones, seeds and flowers and a spiral symbolic of the coil of life. The colour of the east is yellow.

The south is the home of the Plant Kingdom, of the flowers and abundance. It is associated with midheaven, midday, summer. Its element is water and its colour is red. Here were grouped brilliant flowers and red stones.

The west is the home of darkness and eventide. Its element is earth. It is associated with the mineral kingdom, and with harvest, and its colour is black. Here were grouped various dark artefacts, black and grey stones, and also a bear, for bears apparently have an affinity with west.

In the north were grouped various animal figures, for north is linked to the animal kingdom, to winter and to midnight, to the pitch-black time when nature holds her breath. The element associated with north is air.

The slice of the wheel that feels most appropriate to us says something about our essence or our need. For instance, if someone needs to 'sit in the south' it means they need a bit of warmth and passion in their life. But the wheel isn't a strict map of shamanic journey. Like many pagan ideas, thinking of the wheel helps our sense of connection and it is a basis for action and movement, not a creed. It is also beautiful, and the way of the shaman is a path of beauty, a path of balance. The shaman lives in this world, as poet, mystic, wounded healer, but he journeys into the Otherworld and finds inspiration. In a way there is no such thing as a shaman – he is undefinable, he exists in his actions, in his experience. Yet we are to explore something of what it means to be a shaman.

Our guides tell us we are going on an inward journey to find our Power Animal – an animal that symbolises an energy that is helpful to us and we can learn to access. The fragrance of burning sage and sweet-grass fills the air. I feel strangely excited. The candles are lit, the lights go out. We take a deep breath, close our eyes and relax. Now we must imagine simply that we are sitting in a pleasant field. The journey starts as the drum begins to beat.

I cannot remain seated for I am billowed on the drum – beat, beat – down there I see a fox streak out and vanish – beat, beat – like a balloon I'm bobbing, being swept away. I try to return to earth but the drum keeps me above it – beat, beat – up, up I go. I give in to it. How sexual it feels. A really intense physical feeling of the drumbeat deep inside me. I'm riding, dancing, brushing at the edges of ecstasy, but I can't quite let go – beat, beat – I'm soaring by a cliff-top and there is my first power animal, a seagull with three eggs. She leaves them to fly with me on the drum-waves. We are over the sea. There is a lighthouse, shaped like a huge ankh. The light it gives is no ordinary light, searing onto the waves like a laser – beat, beat – and through the waves cuts a saw-shape of a dragon's back. Now the dragon curves around a rock and hatches it like an egg. I don't see what comes out – beat, beat – for my seagull has left, and I bob just above the ocean. The dragon breathes fire upon me. I burn in fear and joy, and then soar in earnest – beat, beat – through a cloud-tunnel towards a great sun-heart, my heart, the world's heart – beat, beat, beat ...

The drum rolls and beats fast. I am hauled in to earth, sad, feeling like clay taken too early from the furnace and still a little clammy. It takes a moment or two to come round. The lights go on and it is time to return to the everyday world. For preference I would have liked the trance to continue for some time, and to have been able to choose when to return. However, this was a memorable experience, because it was extremely vivid and accompanied by strong physical sensations. I now feel I know something at least of what it was like to be a tribal shaman, riven with prophecy, in an agony and an ecstacy of multi-level reality, tearing desperately at shreds of clothing as his being is torn with his primal need to birth the searing vision, to bring the healing ray, to dance the dream alive.

Shamanism — where, what and when

The Medicine Wheel described above is part of the tradition of the American Indians. This is a living tradition, by which I mean it is part of the life and culture of the people, and their daily frame-work. As neo-pagans and witches we tend to live only partially in terms of our spiritual visions, and some of us split off our paganism from segments of our life, either because others wouldn't find it acceptable, or possibly because we just can't keep it up. So we feel a nostalgia about cultures where there is integration. However, there is something distasteful about stealing traditions from a people already dispossessed in other ways and certainly many Native Americans feel rightly incensed at the way some people never initiated into their ways presume to teach their traditions. As this book is about neo-paganism, not about traditions that can claim a completely unbroken line down hundreds of years, this will be our only look at the American Indian. Borrowing is different from stealing, however. The image of the Medicine Wheel is a colourful loan from the most accessible living tradition today, and that is why it is so compelling.

The Amerindians are certainly not the only culture to produce shamanism. *Shaman* is a Siberian Tungusic word meaning 'ecstatic one' (*ex-stasis* from the Greek, meaning altered states of consciousness) and forms of shamanism are, or were found in North and South America, among Australian Aborigines, in Indonesia, China, Tibet and notably Siberia itself. It is arguable that most races at one time in their history had persons who could enter the spirit world and return with valuable information for the tribe. There is a shamanic thread in witchcraft, which claims archaic lineage, and trances can be induced in various ways, by dancing, chanting or by learning to shift consciousness by a mixture of relaxation and visualisation.

The shaman is distinct from a medium, 'channeller' or the ancient Delphic oracle, for instead of the spirit taking over, the role of the shaman is essentially an active one. Shamanic journeys seem almost always to have had a purpose – to discover the origin of problems that may beset the people, such as lack of food or sickness, to help departed or tormented souls or to understand the nature of the breaching of tribal taboos. Unlike the medium, who has no recollection of the spirits who have taken over her or him, the shaman comes back from his journey with a clear memory and precise instructions.

The practice of shamanism is based on the belief that reality has many levels, and the universe consists of a complex energy-network of powers, vibrations and forms, of which the shaman gains direct experience. Most cosmologies used by shamans include three worlds, Upper, Middle and Lower. Usually humans inhabit the middle world, and the three may be linked by a great tree, a sacred river or a road. In Norse mythology the World Tree Yggdrasil grows from the lower world Hel, through Midgard and into the realms of the gods Asgard. For the Siberian Evenks, the three worlds are linked by the Clan River that rises in the upper world where the creator god Amaka lives, also Eksheri, the master of animals, birds and fish, whose good will was needed for good hunting. The lower world is the domain of the dead clansmen, the spirits of disease and of the Clan Mistress, who rules the hunt. The Clan Mistress is half animal, half human, and although the lower world is less pleasant than the upper it is the place of roots, and totemic clan unity stems from there. To become whole we have to seek integration with our darker side and with the things we fear, and the key to full living is strangely hidden in the cave of our deepest terrors. It seems that the shaman would often perform this function of journeying to the forbidden and fearful for the whole tribe, and come back with valuable information for hunt and health.

Although to be a shaman was in a sense a privileged position, it was not usually sought. Rather it seized one, and often arose from a threatening experience such as sickness, assault or a 'near-death' experience. The assumption of the shamanic role was a form of healing, which sounds like a positive use of a disability – the 'wounded healer' archetype. Because of his wounds, his openings to another world, the shaman had access to levels of reality denied to those more whole. Shamanic journeys were dangerous, involving magical dismemberment and rebirth, and possibly one might not return from the spiritual world. Shamans were often helped by spirit guides such as animals or deceased shamans. They were also under potential threat of psychic injury by shamans from opposing tribes, who might be more powerful.

Shamans have been credited in folklore with the power to shape-shift, to go forth in the form of an animal, as witches and sorcerers have been reputed to do. However, in Siberia where the word originated, this was apparently not the case. Accounts of this possibly come from the shamanic ability to merge identity with an animal, or have animal spirit helpers. Drugs were sometimes used by shamans to induce trance states – notably the peyote and San Pedro cacti in South America – and the use of these dates back many thousands of years. There is also the Fly Agaric mushroom that grows over many northern lands. However, it was mostly believed in Siberia that a shaman who needed drugs to go into a trance was second rate. Shamans are by no means always men. In recent history there were often female ones, and there are those who argue that shamanism is most naturally the province of women, and in earlier times when women held more power the shamans were almost always women. A myth of how men long ago stole power from women is told in some variation in all shamanic cultures. The feminine form, *shamanka* is sometimes used.

Shamanism today

It will be obvious that my experience of shamanism had a few things in common with the harrowing journeys of the tribal shaman.

However, it must still be remembered that the shamanic journey has a function. My journey was to find my power animal. There can be several power animals for one person, and it may take several journeys to find them. Discovering them increases a sense of effectuality, and you may surround yourself with images of your power animals to help you in specific situations. Certainly the encounter with mine made me feel protected and energised, and gave me a sense of belonging. It was only days later that I remembered that my maiden name is the Irish-Gaelic for 'seagull', so firmly placing me in the Seagull Tribe!

Workshops, courses and groups that operate today are for the purpose of self-discovery, development and enlightenment, and to enable us to do that magic thing – re-connect. Finding that way of living in harmony with the earth and taking care of Her is so necessary to our well-being. So these journeys do not serve the purpose of ensuring survival of individuals or tribes, but they do keep the vision alive of who we are and where we are going, and the responsibility for the modern shaman is essentially the same: the health and Spirit of the people. Today this may be even more vital, for it could be the survival of humanity that is at stake. A shaman is one who sees that our everyday world is a sort of sleep, that there are brighter levels of existence and all are connected in a web of beingness. Shamanism is a path to true knowledge, it is not about beliefs. Wars are fought over beliefs, never over knowledge.

One of the principal popularisers of shamanism is Carlos Castaneda, author of *The Teachings of Don Juan* and other works. Although the authenticity of his writings has been questioned, it does seem that they are accurate in character, regardless of whether Don Juan – the shaman described in them – 'really' existed or not.

One of the best-known contemporary shamans is Sun Bear. A medicine-man of Chippewa descent he is very New Age in orientation. As a child he had a vision of a large black bear swathed in rainbows, and although he didn't practise the medicine way until he was 25, he now has a huge following. In addition to leading the Bear Tribe in the United States, Sun Bear travels the world giving talks and workshops. Sun Bear draws no salary and does his share of menial tasks on the farm shared with the Tribe. He says, 'We all share the same Earth Mother, regardless of the race ... so let us learn the ways of love, peace and harmony and see the good paths in life.' Sun Bear believes that the Native American teachings have something valuable to offer the world – respect for all of life and balance with the Earth Mother: these are themes central to pagans today.

PRACTICE

If you wish to explore shamanism further there are many opportunities. Some resources and books are listed at the end of this book. The path of the shaman is not a New Age diversion. If truly followed it is a demanding and often lonely vocation, but the potential benefits of bringing the dreams to life and of healing ourselves, others and the earth are great.

Further information

Drury, Nevill, *The Elements of Shamanism*, Element, 1989

Hutton, Ronald, *The Shamans of Siberia*, Isle of Avalon Press, 1993

Matthews, John, *The Celtic Shaman*, Element, 1991

Meadows, Kenneth, *Earth Medicine*, Element, 1989
—— *The Medicine Way*, Element, 1990
—— *Shamanic Experience*, Element, 1991

Sun Bear and Wabun, *The Medicine Wheel*, Prentice-Hall, 1980

Eagles Wing, Centre for Comtemporary Shamanism, 58 Westbere Rd, London NW2 3RU, England. Tel. 0171 435 8174

Different Drum, 71 Painswick Rd, Cheltenham, Glos, GL50 2EX, England

8 ÐRUIÐRY

We sing, we speak poetry, we chant, we make music –
Finding our hearts we have found the heart of the mystery
Finding the depths we have found the Way to be simple

Philip Carr-Gomm, Chief of the Order of Bards,
Ovates and Druids

No one doubts that Druids existed in ancient times, for the
Roman historians speak of them a great deal. However, there
has been much controversy over their history, and about who
qualifies to be called a Druid. Through the years of repression old
pagan ways went underground, and no tradition can claim unbroken
lineage back to the Stone Age – although in this Druidry fares better
than Wicca. Being more 'Apollonian' than witchcraft (philosophical
rather than ecstatic), Druidry has been better accepted in a culture
with values of logic and science. Many erudite and respected men
have been Druids, including William Blake and Winston Churchill.

After a period when the association of Druids with stone circles such
as Avebury and Stonehenge was considered apocryphal, we are now
told that early Druids did worship there. Not that this really matters,
for Druidry is about connecting with the Druid spirit, which is alive
and building bridges of understanding and awareness. Druidry
connects us with the natural world and the sacredness of plant life.
The most likely meaning of Druid is 'Wise man of the oak'.

Levels of Ðruiðry

Training to be a Druid took a long time and I am tempted to believe that many of our forefathers, in days when life expectancy was much less than it is now, must have died in the attempt. There were three levels of Druids – Bards, Ovates and Druids themselves.

Barðs

The Bards were the first grade and working through this could take up to 12 years, after which the student would know hundreds of poems by heart. Bards kept alive the traditions of the tribe in song and composed their own poems – but these were seen as much more than entertainment or historical record. Whoever said 'Sticks and stones may break my bones but words could never hurt me' was insensitive and blind to the evocative power of words to arouse emotions, recall and organise concepts for the memory and understanding, evoke, heal, clarify and command. Words are vibrations and they possess powers that we cannot fully encompass with the logical mind. Poetry and music break down the barriers that consciousness constructs, easing the loneliness of the soul and showing us that we are all one, that we are part of the rolling hills, the tumbling stream and the ancient yew tree. These are values from which we have become estranged, to our cost.

Although placed as the first grade, the Bardic grade lay at the heart of Druidry, for the Bards were masters of creativity. In *The Druid Tradition* Philip Carr-Gomm tells us, 'The Bard's knowledge of and skill with the power of the Word becomes magical with the Druid: understanding the creative force of sound, the Word is used to generate seeds of light that echo through creation.' The Bardic grade is represented by the birch tree and associated with spring and dawn.

Ovates

The second grade was that of the Ovate. Here the initiate learned not only to open the doors of perception, achieved by the Bard, but also those of time itself, and these are shamanic practices. The Ovates were seers, prophets and diviners, working in the realms of death and the spirits of the Ancestors. The lore of trees and herbs was the province of the Ovate, for contact with the plant kingdom connects us to the mysteries of time, death, transformation, sacrifice and rebirth. Plants have many healing properties which the Ovate would have known about, but their more general healing power is what we need to rediscover today – for they show us a way to find connection with the roots of our own beings and find that elusive but simple oneness with nature. The tree of the Ovate grade is the yew, and it is associated with autumn, winter and night – times of reflection and assimilation.

Druids

The third grade was that of the Druid himself. Having made his way through the long and arduous training and having honed his creative powers and his memory and extended his consciousness, the Druid was able to act as judge, philosopher, adviser and teacher. The tree representing the Druid is the oak, and associated with this grade is the east and the times of greatest light and growth – noon and summer. Now, for the Druid the spiral begins anew, reborn through the Bardic Grade and progressing around and upwards, obeying the injunction 'Generate and Regenerate' for life is an ever-growing and changing process and the Druid is both of the ether and of the earth. Concerned with and connected to his environment but fired also by the spirit, the Druid represents much that is relevant to our needs today.

Druids traditionally observe the Eight Festivals. For a Druid the Wheel of the Year and all it tells us about our lives and place on the earth, in nature and the cosmos and the Wheel of Rebirth is as significant as it is to most pagans.

Druidry honours the spirits of the Ancestors as these are the roots from which we have sprung. It also honours the influence of past lives, for though we may not recall them, the memory is lodged in the Unconscious and has links with current experiences we have. This memory is the Spirit of the Journey. Some people seem able to cope with the most dreadful early circumstances and find meaning and purpose in their lives, while others struggle with comparatively minor troubles. These differences can be explained to some extent by the Spirit of the Journey working through the current life. Druids also honour the Spirit of Place – the earth is sacred and certain places are special. There is a quality to Place that is much more than co-ordinates on a map, and feeling a sense of this helps us feel we have a 'place' in the scheme of things. Finally there is the Spirit of Time that we honour when we observe the round of the seasons and the motions of the Moon.

For rituals witches draw a magic circle, invoking the protection of the powers of earth, air, fire and water at the north, east, south and west, in that order. The five Spirits of the Circle of the Druids, as described above, could be linked as follows: Spirit of Place with earth/north; Spirit of the Tribe with east/air (air being connected to the spoken word, and thus to tribal lore), Spirit of Time to the south/fire (where we see the movements of Sun and Moon in the Northern Hemisphere), and Spirit of the Ancestors to west/water (realm of setting Sun, Isles of the Blessed Dead, Waters of healing, remembering, connecting). Thus the Spirit of the journey related to the fifth element, ether, or spirit, that transforms and enlivens from within. You may like to play with other associations and discover meanings for yourself.

Druids have been linked to stone circles, and this is allied to their respect for the Spirit of Place, for these are erected at places of special power on the earth's crust (see Chapter 2). Besides this, the astronomical calculations inbuilt into such structures were important for Druid observances – the truth is 'written in the stones' and there is far more 'truth' here than can be appreciated by measuring and reasoning. However, the Druids are also seen as teaching in groves of sacred trees, and tree lore is significant in Druidry.

Tree Lore

Ogham

We have seen how knowledge of plants was required for the Ovate grade. The Druids built up an extensive system of associations or 'correspondences' connected to trees, called Ogham, and it seems this was as complex and rich as the mystical doctrine of the Qabalah. Each tree was associated with a letter, number, god/dess, mineral, bird, colour, star and so on. This way of thinking about things is very enriching and it seems to bring the world to life, provoking all sorts of ideas, symbols, poetry and inspiration and is a tremendous aid to memory. At first glance it may seem somewhat mechanical, but in practice this is not so at all – it opens up the world and doors to different levels of experience in a way that has to be put into practice to be appreciated. Of course, one doesn't have to stick rigidly to correspondences – they are not intended as a doctrine. Rather they are a ladder or a framework, leading sideways, upwards, downwards and beyond and a structure with which to make sense of inner revelations which might otherwise be unsettling.

It is interesting that Qabalists use the 'Tree of Life' while Ogham uses many trees. Many shamanic cosmologies are based on cosmic trees. Witches riding their besoms has been seen as a metaphor for shamanic journeys, 'riding' a branch of the World Tree (another interpretation of witchy broomsticks!). Our Christmas tree, a mini World Tree or Tree of Life honours these associations at the rebirth time of Yule. Trees are wonderful things and it is small wonder that many people become concerned at their indiscriminate destruction, for they have meanings outside those of environmental concerns.

Mistletoe

Mistletoe has longstanding associations with Druidry. It is a parasitic plant that grows on several trees. It was mistletoe grown on the oak that Druids revered, for they saw this as deeply symbolic. Mistletoe

berries are like semen, and the seeds have not touched the ground –
so they represent potential. Cutting the mistletoe at Yule means
enacting the moment of conception and incarnation. The mistletoe
was cut with a golden sickle – a combination of Sun and Moon,
masculine and feminine, drawing the divine spark down into the
body. As the oak stands for tradition and form and the mistletoe for
spirit, their union is full of mystical significance. The fertility symbolism
of this is obvious, but to the Druids wisdom was important, and so
the mistletoe would have the more esoteric meaning of the Word
made Flesh. This can only be done by the union of opposites, the
complementary, masculine and feminine, Sun and earth.

Druidesses

We have spoken of 'Druids' but there are and were also Druidesses.
Edain McCoy (in *Witta, an Irish Pagan Tradition*, Llewellyn, 1993)
tells us that the Druids in Ireland patriarchalised the older, matrifocal
paganism. We mostly think of the Druids as male, but it depends on
what you call a Druid. Patriarchalisation took place it seems over
most of the world when the *zeitgeist* blew that way. Perhaps the
earlier priestesses can equally well be called Druids. Today it is
certainly a path that is equally open to women, although the largest
organisation, the Ancient Order of Druids, founded by Henry Hurle
in 1781 and associated with much charity work, segregates males
and females into separate lodges – and these are principally male.
However, this order does not teach.

The spread of Druidry

I have not found much information on Druids outside the United
Kingdom, but that doesn't mean they don't exist in some form.
There is a Druid organisation in the United States that grew out of a
tongue-in-cheek protest at the requirement of students at Carleton
College to attend religious services. These Druids worship nature in

groves of trees, celebrate the Eight Festivals, and generally behave as most pagans. They are not alone in having arisen in a spirit of play. Paganism shows that the divine can often be approached in paradoxical ways. It is now becoming generally recognised that the state of mind in which we 'play' is one in which inspiration often flows – hence the term 're-creation': and the Goddess says, 'Let there be "mirth and reverence."'

ḣumɑn sɑcɾiꝼice

Lastly let us address the thorny question of human sacrifice. Druids have been accused of stabbing victims in the method of divination called 'haruspicy' where the flow of blood and death throes were interpreted as augury. There have also been tales of the dreaded wicker men, which were huge man-like frames in which people and creatures were burnt alive, of human sacrifice under oak trees, and more. There is no doubt that many things were practised in the distant past that we would not contemplate today, although how much of this was done by Druids, and how much by the culture of which they were a part is unclear. A Druid standing by, possibly trying to advise, console and modify may have been interpreted as officiating. We all have a savage ancestry, and all religions have carried out reprehensible acts. In this the old pagan ways have been less blameworthy than many other religions. Paganism today is about reclaiming what is best from our past and discovering harmonious ways to go forward.

Further information

Carr–Gomm, Philip, *The Druid Tradition*, Element,1994.
The Order of Bards, Ovates and Druids runs postal courses and workshops. SAE for details from OBOD, PO Box 1333, Lewes, E. Sussex BN7 3ZG. e-mail: oaktreepress @ eworld.com (also *Touchstone* magazine)

The Druid's Voice, Journal of the Council of British Druid Orders, ed. Philip Shallcross, PO Box 29, St Leonards-on-Sea, E. Sussex TN37 7YP

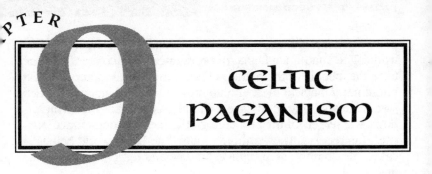

CELTIC PAGANISM

Niamh calling Away, come away:
Empty your heart of its mortal dream.
The wind awaken, the leaves whirl round
Our cheeks are pale, our hair is unbound ...
And if any gaze on our rushing band,
We come between him and the deed of his hand,
We come between him and the hope of his heart.

W.B. Yeats, 'The Hosting of the Sidhe'

Celtic myth and Celtic attitudes are to be found in many current forms of paganism. We have seen that the major festivals of Samhain, Imbolc, Beltane and Lughnasadh are Celtic in origin, and we have looked briefly at one or two Celtic deities such as Cerridwen, Lugh and Brigid. However, there are pagans who follow a path that is specifically and perhaps exclusively Celtic, seeking to reanimate Celtic ways, crafts and terminology and incorporate them in poetry, ritual and life. I say 're-animate' but there is a valid sense in which Celtic ways have remained very much alive, although they are not always appreciated or given due place.

The Irish think of their history mythologically. Stories are told of successive invasions by fantastical divine, or semi-divine peoples. The first of these were the Cessair, followed by the Partholon, the Nemed, Fir Bolg and the Tuatha De Danaan. After these came the Gaels, the first human invaders. Their poet was Amergin, whose Song we shall be looking at later on. These waves of races are described in the twelfth-century Leabhar Gabhala Eireann, or Book of Invasions, and they seem to depict stages in the creation of the world. The Tuatha De Danaan (pronounced *Too-ah day Dawn-ann*) were the 'people of the goddess Dana', the great Mother Goddess. These are a magical race who are now numbered among the faery folk of Ireland, and they have a Cauldron of Abundance which holds the secrets of life and death – the theme of the miraculous cauldron repeats. The Partholon fought the Underworld beings called the Fomhoire – primitive, strange and terrifying one-eyed deities.

Many pagans today use the theme of the quartered circle as a basis for ritual and philosophy. The ancien Irish divided the sacred Land herself into four provinces, with correspondences, as follows:

Leinster: East/Life/Air/Spring/Dawn/Sword (or Arrow)
Muster: South/Light/Fire/Summer/Noon/Spear (or Rod)
Connaught: West/Love/Water/Autumn/Evening/Cauldron (or Cup)
Ulster: North/Law/Earth/Winter/Night/Stone (or Shield or Mirror)

All of the Four Elements are included here, and these are unified by Ether or Spirit. Geographically this was represented by Meath at the centre, the seat of kingship, where stood the royal halls of Tara. It is likely that ancient England, Wales and Scotland had a similar pattern.

Celts from Ireland moved to scotland as late as the 5th century CE (Common Era) arriving in Dalriada, which is now called Argyllshire. A group of present-day Celtic pagans are named the 'clan Dalriada' (see 'Further Resources') and their system includes the lore of the Fir Bolg, Fomhoire, Tuatha De Danaan and the Irish Celts, celebrating light ad dark and seeing everyday life as religious expression.

Celtic history is diffuse, and when we speak of the Celts we are talking about a social and linguistic grouping rather than a strictly tribal and genetic one. The Irish, Welsh and Scots have their own myths, which were transmitted orally for centuries, and these have common themes. The Celts may be thought of as emerging as a recognisable culture in Europe at around 500 BCE. The Celts were savage warriors who collected the heads of their enemies; the sentimental portrayal of them as they fey and dreamy race often favoured today is only partially true. However, heads were hunted for their power and symbology, for the Celts revered eloquence and poetry and respected the potency of the spoken word, which of course issues from the head. The spread of Celtic ways was not due to organised conquest, and indeed Celtic ways often fought each other. It seems Celtic myths, art and religion grew among and within the invaders and the invaded, and were an expression of the development of the collective consciousness of humankind.

We think of celtic peoples as having one foot in the world of Faerie, and to some extent this is true. For instance, to my Irish father the 'little people' were as real as bread and butter. These are the people of the Sidhe (pronounced *shee*) the dwellers in the hollow hills, and there are many folk-tales about them. Celtic people are often credited with having 'second sight' that fades when they leave their native land. However, they are great pragmatists. Their way of going about things may not be the same as the Anglo-Saxon, but they get results. Perhaps it is unease at this that gives rise to so many jokes at their expense!

Some confusion arises about Celtic races even today. Scholars divide them into two major linguistic groups, the P-Celts and the Q-Celts. Q-Celtic is found in Irish Gaelic, Scots and Manx, while P-Celtic (where the sound *q*, *c* and *k* are often replaced with *p*) lives on in Welsh, Breton and the remnants of the Cornish tongue. Celts of different extractions do not always like each other much. Perhaps it is uncomfortable to be comforted by something so like ourselves, yet different enough to be recognised as such. Also Celts are fiercely independent. They have been marginalised and confined but they have never been fully conquered or subsumed, and the Celtic soul paradoxically, is something that is longed for and imitated by races that have tried to subdue, mock or patronise them.

There is a great deal that is relevant to modern pagans in the old Celtic attitudes. For instance, the land was Sovereign Goddess and the King derived his power to rule from Her. If this bond was impaired or violated, sickness and wastage would ensue. This is echoed in the Arthurian myths, which are later forms of much earlier material. The Celts had a profound veneration for Place and to them the land was sacred. Wells, hilltops, trees and other natural features were considered divine. This may have contributed to their defeat by the Romans, for Celtic combat was ritualised and they would not have dreamt of carving up the countryside with earthworks designed to aid them in battle, as did the Roman legions. Today we see that instinct and mysticism are no overt match for linear logic, and yet the victory of the rational is barren – quite literally. The glory that was Rome has decayed, but the poetry and vision of the Celts is very much alive. Although fierce warriors, the Celts often decided battles by single combat. This is echoed in the tale of 'Math, Son of Mathonwy', from the collection of tales called the *Mabinogion*. King Pryderi, having been wronged by the magician Gwydion, faces him in man-to-man contest. Pryderi is slain be Gwydion's magic, but further slaughter among the armies is avoided.

The Celtic calender was constructed according to the Moon, Queen of the night-time. Just as the Celtic year began at Samhain, the start of winter, so too the Celtic day began at nightfall. Darkness was the source, the beginning, Crone come before Maiden, death was inextricably linked to life. We pay lip-service to this, but we are unwilling to accept its implications, for they are painful. Cernunnos, our Horned God, protector of the animals and the instinctual, is depicted by some writers as being linked less to sexual delight, fruitfulness and abandon, than to hunting and culling, purifying and sacrificing. We who find it hard to let go must learn from the bare winter trees, the north wind and the deep, lonely well of midnight, as the Celts did.

By a similar token, the Underworld is seem as a place of regeneration. In the Underworld was a cauldron of rebirth, from which the later Grail legends derive. The cauldron, of course, is a feminine symbol, but also has much to do with transformation, as ingredients are transformed into a brew. The goddess Cerridwen has a magical cauldron. So also does the Daghdha, the great Irish god. The Daghdha was a titanic figure, with a club that conferred life from one tip and death from the other. He is depicted in lusty mating with the death goddess, the morrigan, at Samhain. Here the Morrigan is the 'Washer at the Ford' – the dread apparition that might be seen before battles, washing the armour of those who were to die. He has intercourse with her as she stands astride the River Unius in Connaught. So the god of Life mates with the goddess of Death. This god was often a figure of ribald fun, wearing a tunic that didn't cover his buttocks. So the strands interweave – life and death, sacred and profane, laughter and tragedy, ridicule and wonder. In thinking of the Celts we do well to bear in mind that they did not separate, split and compartmentalise. Their myth was part of their life; inner and outer were the same.

Celtic knotwork is a fascinating and beautiful decorative art. It is also symbolic of Celtic attitudes, for they saw all existence as linked – actions and reactions, life and the individual, Otherworld, Underworld, the Everyday, person, god/dess and place all intertwine in an endless web. Tweak any part, however gently, and the entire network resonates in harmony. As the Gaels land on the Irish shore, at Beltane, their bard, Amergin, delivers a beautiful pagan litany:

> I am a stag: of seven tines ...
> I am a hill: where poets walk,
> I am a boar: ruthless and red,
> I am a breaker: threatening doom ...
> I am an infant: who but I
> Peeps from the unhewn dolmen arch?

This is a many-faceted statement, but clearly the bard, the people, the animals, plants and the land, the fearsome, the beautiful, the wise and the innocent are declared as one, and celebrated. As we wear Celtic knotwork today, in jewellery, we can let out minds follow th twisting, delving path it represents, back into the magical world that was then, and that still exists.

Originally Celtic myths were preserved orally, and there were many different goddesses and gods, associated with different locations – stream, wells grove. And yet a traveller could recognise familiar deities even though they might be called by a different name. Pantheons were not unified and unchanging. The ancient mother goddesses were terrifying as much as nurturing, and goddesses were considered more powerful than gods, from their relationships with the land. Women, too, were powerful and respected, and succession was matrilinear. Gentle pagans of today no doubt have little in common with the wild, painted and armed Celtic warrior, and yet there is so much about the Celts that speaks of what we seek now. How then do we reclaim it?

In *The Pagan Index*, John H. T. Davies comments: 'As a native born Welshman who loves his country ... I am worried about this fashion ... for "Celtic Shamanism" ... our spiritual heritage may be ... insensitively exploited ... a kind of spiritual strip mining.' He continues eloquently on the subject of sentimentalising the Celts and using their mythology and traditions without understanding them. He also makes it clear that no true entry can be gained to the Celtic world by those not born to it. However, entry to the Otherworld, to the place so vivid and yet so misty, to the breathtaking beauty, the savagery, the twists and turns, the paradox and the magic can be gained by approaching it with open hearts and with humility. 'Don't invoke anything according to what you already know' John Davies tells us. 'Wait gently for whatever is there to touch you in its own way.'

So, to find the Celtic soul, go to where the pewter sea shatters against scarred rock, go to where the mist spirals, to some forest place smelling of moss and secrets. Curl in the claw of a tree-root, stand on a cliff-top and face the grey sky, or listen to the many-tongued mountain stream. Go to find your goddesses and gods, don't take them with you as shapes, pre-formed and pretty, but let them speak to you out of the land. As John Davies says '... what you get will not be what you expect.'

Further information

Graves, Robert, *The White Goddess*, Faber & Faber, 1988

Jones, G. and T. (Trans.), *The Mabinogion*, Everyman, 1989

McCoy, Edain, *Witta, an Irish Pagan Tradition*, Llewellyn, 1993

Matthews, Caitlin and John, *Hallow Quest*, Aquarian, 1990
——— *The Arthurian Tarot*, Aquarian, 1992
Powerfully evocative Tarot Pack. The book and pack are a basis for inner journeys based on Arthurian myths. The pack alone comes with an informative instruction book.

Sharkey, John, *Celtic Mysteries*, Thames & Hudson

Stewart, R.J., *Celtic Gods, Celtic Goddesses*, Blandford, 1990

Toulson, Shirley, *The Celtic Alternative*, (Shirley Toulson Books)

Clan Dalriada (postal courses) 2 Brathwic Pl. Brodick, Is of Arran

House of the Goddess, Celtic Hs. 33 Oldridge Rd, London SW12 8PN

Irish Pagan Movement, Bridge Hs. Clonegal, Enniscorthy, Co. Wexford, Eire

Centre of Pandora/Pan, Blaenberem, Mynyddcerrig, Llanelli, Dyfed SA15 5BL

THE NORTHERN TRADITION

I know that I hung on a windswept tree,
Swung there nights all nine ...
Down to the depths I peered
To take up the Runes
With a roaring scream.

The Havamal

The Northern Tradition is inspired by Norse and Anglo-Saxon myths. It is dramatic and dynamic, and growing in popularity. Followers are often called heathens rather than pagans. They believe that it is natural to follow gods that inspired our forbears. In the Norse mythology there are just as many goddesses as gods (more than 100, to my knowledge) and one of the main differences between Asatru (the worship of the Aesir deities) and other pagan paths is that the male and female elements are regarded as exactly equal in power. The Vikings have been rather unfairly linked with rape and pillage because their activities were documented by monks who were among their victims, whereas the Celts and others who were equally warlike have fared better. However, Peter Jennings tells us (*Talking Stick Magickal Directory*); 'Positive attributes in Norse society include jewellery and poetry ... a highly developed and much copied legal system and a self-sufficient, honourable and pioneering outlook.' The horned helmets associated in the popular imagination with Viking bestiality were in fact never worn in combat, and donned only for ritual purposes – in fact reminiscent of the Horned God.

Deities

Norse deities are divided between the Vanir, who are nature spirits, and the more clearly defined Aesir. The faith itself is called Asatru, or Odintru, for the god Odin is its principal inspiration. The Anglo-Saxons called him Woden, and he has given his name to Wednesday. Deities are divided equally between male and female, and women had considerable status among the Norsemen, having the right, in the words of Jennings, 'to vote, divorce, and own land long before their modern British counterparts'. Many women are currently attracted to the Norse tradition although it seems less Goddess-orientated than most other pagan paths. Followers tend to reject 'armchair heathenism' in favour of pursuing environmental initiatives, such as protecting badgers or yew trees, and involvement in national campaigns.

Runes and the Tree of Life

'Central to all Northern Traditions thought and magic', writes Jennings, 'are the runes and the image of the world ash tree, Yggdrasil, a tree of life symbol with nine worlds.' These nine worlds are as follows: Midgard, the land of ordinary mortals; Asgard, land of the Aesir; Hel, the world of the Dead; Vanaheim, home of the Vanir and Freya's Hall; the land of Fire, the land of the Light Elves, the land of the Dark Elves, the land of the Ice Giants and the land of Fog. Nine is a number of great symbolic importance in Asatru, as it was to the Celts. The runes are mystical symbols used in magic, descriptively, as an alphabet, and in divination in a way similar to the Tarot. Odin hung on the world tree, Yggdrasil, for nine days to learn the secret of the runes in a shamanic experience.

Odin discovering runes hanging on world tree

Magic, Ritual and Myth

There are three types of Norse magic: Seidr, intuitive, herbalistic and shamanistic, Galdr, the written and spoken ritualistic side and Taufr, which deals with talismans. The goddess Freya (goddess of love and beauty who has given her name to Friday) imparted the secrets of Seidr to Odin. Seidr is practised by the Volva, a seeress, and the Grimsrular, who are shamanic priests. There are also Gothi and Gotha – community priests and priestesses, who practise Galdr and Taufr. These are still alive within the Northern Tradition. Like most other pagan systems, rituals are adapted from other methods and suited to a modern approach. The Vikings themselves were a people who looked to the future.

Odinists usually celebrate at Full Moon and the eight seasonal festivals, but there are variations in the mythology. For instance, at Yule, which is the Norse New Year, the myth of the beautiful god Baldur is remembered. Baldur is the Sun God, who is plagued by awful dreams of death. So Freya, his mother goes around the world getting every living thing to promise not to harm him, which they readily do, for everyone loves the Sun. The gods amuse themselves by flinging anything and everything at the now invincible Baldur. However, Loki, god of mischief, discovers that the only living thing overlooked has been the mistletoe, being too young and insignificant to cause harm. Disguised as an old woman, he whispers in the ear of poor, blind Hlod, Baldur's brother, and persuades him to join the game. He guides his hand as he flings a spear of mistletoe at Baldur, who falls down and dies.

Now the Aesir and all of creation are plunged into mourning. Odin sends to the realms of the goddess Hel, who says she will return Baldur to the upper world if everything alive cries for the Sun god. Tears fall all over the world, but the only person who refuses to cry is a grumpy old giantess, who is Loki in disguise. So Baldur must remain for ever in the land of shadows. Loki is discovered and pays a terrible penalty, chained in the bowels of the earth, while poison from a serpent drips unendingly on him. His shakes and screams are the cause of earthquakes, and so he will writhe until the end of the world.

This is a no-nonsense myth which puts us in touch with endings. Of course we know that Baldur must be born again or the Sun would never return. However, to experience death and darkness the ending must feel final, for only in this way can a transformation take place. Loki represents the necessary force of destruction, without which there can be no true change or growth – and it is interesting that he is an androgynous figure, habitually dressing up as women, who in this story are rather crone-like. In a way it seems unfair that he should suffer so badly, but his power is in no way diminished, manifesting as earthquakes and tremors which shake the foundations of all security.

ORGANISATIONS

Sources for Odinists are not as plentiful as for some other traditions, being principally the Eddas, two books written in Iceland after its Christianisation, plus the rune poems and other fragments. Some consider this a good thing, for Odinists are not restricted as Wiccans are, being free to be creative and inventive, within the spirit of their tradition. Also they have to think carefully about their rituals and ethics, because there are no prescribed ways to follow, which encourages independence and responsibility, in the Viking tradition. Odinists organise themselves into 'hearths' or work solo. Some have a variety of ritual equipment, like Wiccans; others have little more than a candle. Some wear robes, or go sky-clad if everyone is happy this way, but many just wear their ordinary clothes. Magic is not necessarily worked, for some Odinists are happy merely to celebrate their religion. There is a preference for conducting rites outdoors in groves of trees where possible, preferably of ash, oak and hazel.

There is no system of hierarchy or degrees, just one Hearth Guardian who oversees the setting up of the group. However, there is an umbrella organisation called Odinshof, a registered charity, founded in 1987, whose aims are to promote awareness of Odin's ancient teachings and philosophy. It is run by the Witan Assembly, and has several hundred members in Britain and abroad. The Witan Assembly has a grading of Odal and Oak. New members start at Odal and are promoted to Oak after 13 moons if they have proved themselves worthy and achieved experience.

PRACTICE

Those interested in exploring the Northern Tradition may like to contact some of the groups listed at the end of this book and to delve further into the riches of the tradition by reading some of the books also listed here. This is certainly a lively, growing and active branch of paganism.

Further information

Arcarti, Kristyna, *Runes for Beginners*, Hodder & Stoughton, 1994

Aswynn, Freya, *Leaves of Yggdrasil*, Llewellyn

Crossley-Holland, Kevin, *Norse Myths*, Penguin

Pennick, Nigel, *Practical Magic in the Northern Tradition*, Aquarian

Gippeswic Magazine, 42 Cemetery Rd, Ipswich, Suffolk IP4 2JA

Odinsof, BM Tercel, London, WC1N 3XX, England

The Rune Gild. Open to all those who feel they have true 'contact' with the Northern Folksoul. To study the esoteric path of the runes, correspondence courses available. Write with a short introduction about yourself. Rune Gild UK, BM Aswynn, London, WC1N 3XX, England.

FEMINISM

I am Woman, midnight seer
Darkened mirror, crystal clear
Wise owl eye, eagle wing
Fiery tongue, now hear me sing
Ayi, Ayi
Now hear me
Now hear me

I Am Woman

Paganism is very much about Goddess worship, and so is implicitly feminist. However, for many pagans this worship is not enough. They feel that all things feminine have been denied, and that merely to reinstate the Goddess with all Her attendant myths, does nothing for the cause of women and very little for feminine spirituality. Some Wiccan high priestesses are seen as maintaining a 1950s lifestyle in which they have little real power as people, and compensate for this by ruling their covens with a rod of iron. In this way Goddess-worship acts like a sop – Marx's 'opiate of the masses' – and serves more to keep women away from real power. Something more radical is called for, where female spirituality is integrated with true feminine effectuality. Patriarchy has valued woman as Mother or Virgin, but never as free spirit, mistress of her own destiny and sexuality. Many women now choose not to have children and to be free to explore other forms of creativity. Pagan values cherish this as much as the biological forms of creation and nurture.

aug 24 · virgo · sept 23

the sign may have derived from the...

a mutable sign - versatile & responsive

...ruled by the planet ⚥ ☿ · an earth sign · practical & committed

great goddess as earth mother & sacred virgin ⚥

virgo associations ~ hazel · zircon · violets · dark moon ·

associated with the goddesses demeter & persephone ⚥

ŋ energy ~ skilful · thoughtful · analytical · sincere · refined

lavender · cypress · jasper · autumn equinox · corn flowers

⚥ symbolised by the corn-maiden ⚥

path of clarity

Virgo

99

Separatism

This view has influenced pagan spirituality in several ways. There are Dianic covens, composed of women only, and some are lesbian groups. For some women this is mainly for comfort and ease – there are usually more women in covens than men, and women on their own are often more co-operative. Rituals may be more powerful because they arise from true consensus and evolve at whatever pace is necessary. For others who feel more militant, men may be seen as undesirable and therefore excluded. Worship of the Goddess is foremost and some groups follow what may amount to Goddess monotheism. However, whether militant feminists or 'ordinary' wives and mothers, most pagan women are confident and personally powerful without belligerence, relating to men as friends and lovers while still promoting women's issues within paganism and the world at large.

There is no doubt that many women have been severely bruised by men and the patriarchy. There is no denying the huge rage resulting from this, that probably affects all of us – women and men. We have all, whether we realise it or not, been damaged in ways we are only just beginning to guess by a world-view that is implicitly anti-matter/the flesh/the inclusive/the instinctual: all that women may be seen to stand for. I say 'may be' because I don't think we can really be sure exactly what women do stand for, nor what men stand for, which is something we can begin to discover only by having a very open mind.

For women who so wish, the value of all-female covens is undeniable. Some of the liveliest spirit of the current pagan movement comes from women's groups, who find a tremendous source of freedom and inspiration in Goddess worship and female companionship and see no need for the so-called 'creative polarity' that runs between male and female. Or they see this creative polarity as being present in all-women groups anyway.

However, for most feminists the matter by no means rests there. For religious observance without political action is only part of the story. To 'render unto Caesar the things that are Caesar's and unto God the things that are God's' is just one of the paralysing, distorting splits of the Judaeo-Christian tradition. For wholeness they feel we must campaign actively for women's rights, using our spirituality to galvanise, not to distract. So women's groups are perhaps more likely to concern themselves with community and environmental issues and with active political campaigning, without which they see no real change can take place. This seems to be especially so in the United States.

The witch in every woman

It can be said that every woman is a witch at heart, if we peel back the layers to the black rose at the centre. Womanliness is about wild strawberries, honey and lilies; but it is also about garlic, nightshade, compost, the coil of the cobra, the siren's song and the flutter of the bat's wings at midnight. Such have often been linked to the sinister, but there is no evil here, except to those determined to see it that way. However, there is certainly something scary. It threatens the sterilised, logical world-view as much as that view has threatened it – and after centuries in dungeons, rubbish tips and blazing pyres it is very, very angry. The stately Goddess-worship of Wicca opens the doors to this, but does not really express it in its full savagery and beauty.

In the past witches have been creatures of the fringes, working for the cause of the repressed, linking hands with Romanies, outcasts and tramps in a soft-footed tarantella of apostasy. We have always needed forces for change, although they are anathema to the repressive die-hard and so the 'burning times' can be seen as political suppression as well as religious. However, in common with many pagans, feminist witches believe that matriarchy was once generally upheld, and that it was radically different from patriarchy, meaning much more than substituting a woman-at-the-top for a man-at-the-top.

Matriarchy upholds female values, working inclusively and non-controllingly, valuing the sensual and the spontaneous in a way that structured masculinity does not. One of the realms of experience that is especially feminine – that of menstruation – has been denigrated by patriarchy. A matrifocal culture would have valued the time of the menses and segregated menstruating women not because they were 'dirty' but because they were especially powerful and important at this sensitive time. Especially, a matrifocal culture values the experience of childbirth, and the caring and realism this creates. And women who do not have children are able to bring the passion and nurture of their femaleness into other creative areas. Witches of today are no longer necessarily secret. Often hard-working and by most definitions ordinary, having families and jobs they are working peaceably but steadily to see the power of women re-rooted and growing healthily.

FEMININITY

It seems that despite decades of 'women's lib' very little has been done to liberate true femininity, or even to discover what it is. The women who have achieved power are often more masculine than the male, damaging rather than championing women's issues. Women now undeniably have more opportunity to compete head to head with men in the workplace and that has given rise to a whole new range of problems. So now they are free to join the bald heads and coronaries and to pay some presumably less 'liberated' woman to look after their children. Women now have greater pressures in some ways, almost forced into the role of breadwinner through divorce, or by husbands' inability to get jobs – sometimes because they are being given to women. Many are faced with a heartbreak they had not imagined (because until one has given birth one can't) of leaving their babies with childminders when their maternity leave comes to an end. Is that any closer to freedom than being 'stuck at home'? Until we examine our culture and language closely, we cannot fully realise how deeply denegration of the feminine is rooted. Even committed Goddess worshippers exclaim 'For God's sake!' or 'Oh God'. To be called a 'tomboy' is considered a compliment: 'big girl's blouse' definitely is not.

A WAY FORWARD

here are no easy answers to these dilemmas, but the pagan way of
respecting the past, traditions and ancestors, and a matrifocal
attitude gives us some clues. Doubtless there was much in the old
ways that would be unpalatable to us now, and dreams of a golden
age are misleading. But what about sisterhood – groups of women
supporting each other in raising families and creative work? And
what about a radical Goddess-inspired shift in attitude, where
children are catered for and accepted in the workplace? After all,
who says we have to be so formal? The way of the Goddess does
not say that women have to become men. At this time She sends us
on a quest to find what we really are and can do and to ask
questions – some perhaps superficial, others more troubling.

I'd like to leave this subject with a passage from the feminist group
WITCH ('Women's International Terrorist Conspiracy for Hell' or
Women Incensed at Telephone Company Harrassment' – the name
changes to suit needs!) This is an American group quoted by Margot
Adler in *Drawing Down the Moon*:

> *If you are a woman and dare look within yourself you are a*
> *Witch. You make your own rules. You are free and beautiful ...*
> *Your power comes from your own self as a woman, and it is*
> *activated by working in concert with your sisters ...*
> *You are a Witch by saying aloud 'I am a Witch' three times,*
> *and THINKING ABOUT THAT. You are a witch by being*
> *female, untamed, angry, joyous and immortal.*

Further information

Bohen, Jean, *Goddesses in Everywoman*, Harper & Row, 1984

Pinkola-Estes, Clarissa, *Women who Run with the Wolves*, Rider, 1994

Shan, *Circlework*, House of the Goddess, 1994

Starhawk, *Dreaming the Dark*, Beacon Press, 1982

12

tbe men's movement

I am a stag: of seven tines
I am a flood: across a plain
I am a wind: on a deep lake
I am a tear: the sun lets fall.

Song of Amergin, restored by Robert Graves

Not surprisingly the Woman's Movement and Goddess worship present men with some problems. Many sensitive men feel a burden of responsibility and guilt over the hurt done to women and things feminine over the ages and they are not sure how to compensate for this, or what their role as men can be in a Goddess-centred religion. This is not to say that they have a problem with Goddess worship itself. Loving the earth, discovering the gentle, the spontaneous and instinctual in themselves and treasuring it in their partners, they find that the Goddess beckons them.

However, women are also wild, free and assertive. They embody dark Crone as well as brighter aspects, and the Goddess can be the deep cauldron, the sow that eats her farrow. These elements are not very acceptable to men generally and may be hard to absorb for those discovering their softer side. Does this mean they should become subordinate to strong women?

Some men pay lip-service to equality and the Goddess, and still leave all the housework to their wives. Others are saddened by their exclusion from women-only groups. Yet others subordinate hemselves to a priestess – who may also be their wife – without having truly found anything new that enriches them as people and males. Do women really want a race of submissive males carrying their handbags and doing nothing but washing floors and looking after the children? Surely the answer has got to be no, for then Great Pan would be well and truly dead.

What paganism truly offers men is the opportunity to be multi-faceted. Not a wimp, but not the stern aggressor either. It offers the possibility of going on a quest for the true self and essential maleness that is not bound by stereotypes such as the 'stiff upper lip', or the 'master of the house'. For this it offers models in the divine – such as Pan himself – where the instinctual is combined with masculine strength, where gentleness and protectiveness do not mean weakness, and where the Wild Man has as much place as the Wild Woman, the Witch.

Iron John

In response to the Women's Movement some men have started to form groups of their own and one of the sources of inspiration is the fairy-tale of Iron John. Iron John is a seemingly sinister figure discovered rusting in a pool in the forest and supposedly responsible for the disappearance of travellers. When he is found he is put in chains and kept in a cage in the castle, a sad, lonely figure. One day the Prince's ball strays into the cage and Iron John refuses to return it unless he is released. The Prince hesitates and then goes to get the key to the cage which happens to be hidden under his mother's pillow. Iron John escapes, taking the Prince with him on his shoulders and looks after him in the woods. However, the young, inexperienced Prince fails certain tests and so he cannot stay with Iron John. He has to go and make his way by toiling on his own, but Iron John comes to his aid when he needs him. Eventually through acts of valour he marries a Princess, and Iron John is reinstated with honour.

In common with all myths the above can be interpreted and

reinterpreted, found to mean many things or just seen as an interesting story. For me one of the important points seems to be that the key to the release of this Wild Man is under the Queen's pillow. So the Prince finds the first real contact with Iron John through searching in a secret and personal space of his mother's. Men can find the 'key' hidden in a feminine place within, in their sleeping sensitivity, in their vulnerability and weakness, in their unconscious. However, it doesn't stop there. The Prince doesn't go and hide in his mother's bed. He takes what he finds under her pillow and opens doors to the rest of his life. I take this to mean that self-discovery, for men, may start by exploring their feminine side and making use of it, but that is just the start. At the end of the journey is a man who is truly brave, for he is not afraid to feel, to serve, to toil, to remain hidden and to work with his own instinctual side as represented by the Wild Man, Iron John. His reward is integration and the reinstatement of the wild side as a source of power – marriage with the Princess and the companionship of Iron John, who is left to rust no more.

Iron John, the Green Man, the Horned God – these are just some of the figures that can help a man in pagan spirituality, and pagan resources are as rich for men as for women, for those who decide to seek within them. The true pagan male is helpful and supportive, for masculine strength needs to be used in service to and protection of the generative and creative forces, whether simply in the Goddess or embodied in wife and family. But loving service is not subordination. We do not want a pendulum-swing where men are relegated to the downtrodden position women have occupied for centuries – despite the little voice that sometimes pipes up 'Serve them right!' The idea has got to be self-realisation and appreciation for all, and that is something to work towards.

homosexuality

Homosexuality is a force within paganism too, and just as there are covens of lesbian women, so there are groups of homosexual men, wishing to celebrate their sexuality as a gift of the Goddess. This is more than coming out. It is seeing one's own sensuality as holy and having the opportunity to meet other men who value themselves and the love they have to give in the same way. Homosexual pagans sometimes point out that homosexuality has been associated with shamanism, and that the homosexual experiences a greater unity of the sexes within himself than does the heterosexual, who is looking for a partner to complement her/him. It is also said that gays were burnt along with witches – hence the term 'faggot'.

The true spirit of paganism today is to value 'all acts of love and pleasure' and to find valid ways of honouring the Goddess and God within us all and within the earth. The way of the Goddess gives unfettered life to all that is vital, beautiful and meaningful. It does not separate, judge, compare or select, but it asks that we be true to ourselves. That is no small task.

Further information

Bly, Robert, *Iron John*, Element, 1992

Hoblink. For gay & bisexual pagans. SAE Box 22 'Out' Bookshop, 4–7 Dorset St. Brighton, BL2 1WA England

13

ECO-PAGANS AND CYBER-PAGANS

You were born of Her, She gave you being
She healed your body and brought your soul fire
When the Mother wakes we must awaken with Her
We will fade away if we let Her die

Carolyn Hillyer, 'Tread Gently' from the album *House of the Weavers* and the book *Two Drumbeats: Songs of the Sacred Earth*, Seventh Wave Music, 1993

ECOLOGY

Love for the Earth is part of the pagan soul. We take from the bounty of the Earth gladly, and give back with equal pleasure. There are links between pagans and the environmental lobby in Britain and the States, but these are less definable in Australia, where certain members of the pagan movement are eager to see such bonds forged. This has been called 'eco-paganism' or 'green spirituality' and is growing greatly in momentum. If paganism is a way of life, then that way of life needs to take into account the welfare of all creatures on Earth, and of the earth herself. Green spirituality is so much a part of true paganism that it hardly needs to be stated. It also seems to be common sense and sound survival instinct.

In *Gaia* (Oxford, 1987) J. E. Lovelock writes: 'It does not seem inconsistent with the Darwinian forces of evolutionary selection for a sense of pleasure to reward us by encouraging us to achieve a balanced relationship between ourselves and other forms of life.' In other words he is saying that loving nature is a survival instinct. However, it is one that we have almost lost, suppressed by worship of science and the urge to 'progress'. Many pagans are passionate about nature, and have risked life and limb to protect areas of beauty from the bulldozer.

Trees arouse many feelings in sensitive people, who have fought to preserve them. They are heavy with symbolism, as the Tree of Life, as World Tree, in Ogham correspondences. They are beautiful as poised dancers over hill and valley, and they are useful for their wood, fruits and their contribution to the atmosphere. But they are something much more, something that we cannot fully encompass. This quotation from Terry Pratchett's *The Colour of Magic* (Corgi, 1983) expresses this in part: 'Do you not know that what you belittle by the name tree is but the mere four-dimensional analogue of a whole multi-dimensional universe?' Pagans express their love and respect for trees by asking the tree if they may cut a branch, and thanking it afterwards. Of course, if you ask you must listen with your inner ear for the answer.

It is often unclear exactly what is harmful to the environment and what isn't. Scientists argue, and are sometimes suspected of leaning towards views that support whoever happens to be paying them. Emotions run high among environmental pressure groups, who cannot bear to see another slice of hillside carved up, or another river polluted beyond all recognition. This may not always be reasonable, but it is understandable. Perhaps what we are needing to salvage is something in ourselves as much as nature – that wild and free spirit, of which civilisation and the de-souling of nature has robbed us.

The earth has withstood many huge changes in her lifetime and none of these have destroyed her – although sometimes many life-forms perished during climatic adjustments. Probably the worst harm we can do would be to render this beautiful world uninhabitable by us and many other species but Gaia would survive. J. E. Lovelock has put forward a reasoned argument for considering the earth sentient and self-regulating, which he says country people have always known. In some ways anything we do is 'natural' for we are children of Gaia. In another sense even living is unfriendly to the environment, for we all produce methane – a greenhouse gas – along with many other polluting qualities of our bodies. So what on earth do we do?

As usual the answer is probably one of balance. We should not decide to stop living as we know it, give up all the comforts of civilisation and return to tribal ways – we could hardly do this even if we wanted to. However, we should proceed with respect and common sense, and with awareness attempt an attunement with our mother the earth. We probably need our instincts as much as anything else for this, for years of environmental science have supplied few definite answers. However, this is as much a matter of our spiritual well-being as our physical, for unless we respect the earth we cannot properly respect ourselves or our fellows. A little true deference for nature will do more than pages of equations and formulae, and we can all undertake some simple environmental measures. We shall be looking at these in more detail at the end of the chapter.

However, practical measures are not the whole story, for many pagans perform eco-magic. These are rituals for general earth healing, or for specific environmental or humanitarian causes. The energy of the earth that we discussed in Chapter 2 may be raised and focused to the objective in question. This is done responsibly and positively, for the object is to help the earth and the life upon her, not to harm the polluters.

Technology

If Gaia is a living, sentient creature, then we who are part of her have a function within her system. Lovelock suggests that mankind may be a 'Gaian nervous system' and a part of her development: through us she can reach into space, through us she can become conscious of herself, and through us she may have a chance to survive the type of event that could otherwise devastate her – for example a collision with a meteor. Our advancing technology might prevent this as nothing else could, providing, for example, the only imaginable positive use of the atom bomb.

Technology is certainly not all harmful, although pagans can be divided on this subject. Some favour the 'back-to-nature' approach, but there are some who tried it and found it can be uncomfortable and joyless. Some are suspicious of technology, but others embrace it as being very much in keeping with a world-view that gives room to all possibilities, and see computers as a type of magic. Computers are very much part of modern technology. Love them or hate them – and it is characteristic of pagans to do either or both – it seems they are here to stay and to grow in significance.

What can this mean in practice? Computers do offer something positive environmentally: they are clean and use very little power. More than this, however, they may provide a way of living and working that takes away the pressing need for that most polluting thing, the motor car. There is a special place for computers in a world wishing to retrieve community values, to save energy and to encourage communication and cross-fertilisation between groups and nations.

Through video-conferencing, a computer can enable participation in meetings and organisation without ever having to get into a car, and although not readily available as yet, this is becoming more accessible. Working on a computer one can have access to all the records one might need and can communicate with a central office without leaving the desk in the study at home – and soon it will be possible to do most of the shopping by similar methods. However, this does not mean a nation of lonely square-eyes, punching keyboards in back rooms. On the contrary it offers the possibility of a new sense of community and place, of interacting with one's neighbours and developing a feeling of roots that cannot be achieved spending half of one's life at work, miles from home, or commuting. More than this, telecottages – computer centres available to those who do not have access to the same equipment at home – again offer a fresh 'village' arrangement, a place for get-togethers and access to vast storehouses of information – all in a way most friendly to the environment and community and in keeping with a pagan spirit.

Besides this, computers offer access to the information superhighway – a global forum for sharing, swapping and storing information. Pagans already make full use of this, for there is an immense amount of data on wicthcraft and paganism available on the Internet. More than this, people who are interested, puzzled or doubtful about any subject can have ready contact with others who know more and are able to supply information and discussion first hand, in a way that is safe, doesn't commit anyone and dissolves boundaries. This is invaluable in the case of paganism and related topics, for ignorance and prejudice tend to disappear where barriers are impossible to maintain – and there is no way of 'policing' the Internet, as yet.

In addition to the practical benefits of the information superhighway, some occultists perceive this as something greater than the sum of its parts – a change in and a step up for the energies of the planet, a force for alteration in consciousness. It is widely believed that we are entering the Age of Aquarius. Aquarius is ruled by Uranus, the planet of electricity, of invention and innovation. All these are exemplified by the World-Wide Web.

Witches are weavers, and if we are wise we weave into the tapestry of life without pulling threads. Celtic knotwork is an artistic expression of the intricacies of the web of life, the many inter-connections, the pattern of existence, death, rebirth – the continuing thread. In some strange way the Internet, the web of energy and communication around the globe into which anyone who can get to a terminal can 'sew a thread', partakes of these concepts. It is an abstract that we have access to, but which we can never completely encompass at any one time. It is a creation of science, yet it is something more. It offers us a possible expansion of experience, of new dimensions – it can be a chance for real change for humanity, as any person who reaches into the Web is part of something much greater, and gives to something greater, however small a part that may be.

And so we have 'cyber-pagans' – those who are very well attuned to the possibilities offered by computers and the information superhighway as well as the old, deep energies of Mother Earth. Like the Roman god Janus (who gave his name to January) we need to have two faces – one that looks backwards to our ancient past, and another that looks forwards to a New Age that isn't 'just crystals and light' but is the real dawning of a new consciousness. Maybe we can complete the circle. Having left our roots, our instincts and tribal ways to develop a sense of logic, reason and science, perhaps we can now reconnect with these roots: not rejecting all we have learned along the way, but respecting intuition and sense of origin and combining it to use the best our science has produced – in a sense to come back to our place of origin and to know it for the first time. Then we will truly have a New Age – an inspiring thought!

We can now look at some very simple practical ways of looking after the environment. Many of these I am sure you will be familiar with and may be doing already, so if I'm preaching to the converted I apologise. Of course, each person on their own makes little difference, but that doesn't mean there is no point in trying – for to take that attitude is to partake of despair at modern life. After all, from tiny acorns grow large and long-lived oak trees.

PRACTICE

- Don't buy rubbish. Many products are vastly over-packaged, with bits of cardboard and plastic that could well be done without. Choose products with as little wrapping as is practical.
- Recycle where possible. I know there is debate about which uses more resources, recycling or not, but at least recycling means we don't have to bury masses of rusty tins. There are usually recycling sites at supermarkets. Keep all your tins, bottles, jars, paper and old clothes in bags in a clean bin and just take them with you when you do the shopping. Children are often very helpful with this.
- Compost where possible. Even if you aren't going to use it on a garden it is better to let organic matter rot naturally than have it carted off to a tip. Have a special bin for it if you like – a couple of added yarrow leaves will speed up the composting.
- Use the car less. Walk or cycle where it is safe and practical. Car-share. Fit a catalytic converter, but remember that for short journeys it makes no difference – walking will make you healthier and be better for the air.

- Save power. Proper insulation, low energy light-bulbs and turning the central heating down a couple of degrees will save money, too.
- Be a 'joiner' – some relevant organisations are listed below. Of course not all change is bad change. Environmental pressure groups may make mistakes as anyone can, but the important thing is they make people think. Joining an organisation will give a focus to your efforts – but if you feel more militant, be a leader yourself.
- Look around your own locality. Are there dumps that could be cleaned up, streams that could be cleared? Maybe your local Guides, Brownies, Cubs and Scouts would be interested in doing this.
- Get organised! Otherwise you will end up buying whatever is most convenient. Ten minutes of thinking about exactly what you are going to buy and where, is invaluable. Soon it will become a habit, and you won't have to plan.
- Think about what you eat. It is not sustainable for the world's population to eat meat daily, and many animals are reared in dreadful conditions. You may like to reduce the amount of meat in your diet, look for free-range, organic meat or be entirely vegetarian. Some pagans feel you should only eat an animal that you have killed, at least once, as in this way you are honouring the life-force of the animal and facing up to what you are doing. A list of organic meat producers is obtainable from the Soil Association.
- Don't wear a hair shirt! Caring for the environment shouldn't be a chore, an obsession or be uncomfortable or dangerous. Don't risk cycling on very busy roads or shiver in an unheated house. I don't think that is the way of the Goddess, and it will just put everyone off who comes in contact with it.

These are some suggestions from me, but you can make up your own mind, and if it is important to you and you give yourself the chance to 'tune in' you will know what is right for you to do. You can do some eco-magic of your own, if you wish. Simply save a few crumbs at the end of a meal and strew them outside, saying with awareness, 'I return a gift to my Mother, with love.' Stand outside in the sunshine.

Let the warmth fall upon you, within you. Feel the glow gathering in power and warmth behind your navel. When you are ready hold out your arms and let the healing energies flow outwards. Visualise them healing the earth, revitalising the soil. Imagine this clearly, then let go. You may do the same on a windy day, taking a deep breath of the wild air and breathing out, imagining the wind sweeping away all harm. Similarly with rain, if you don't mind getting wet. Imagine the cleansing energies of the rainwater taking away pollutants, beautifying the land. These small rituals will be more effective if undertaken at a place that is special to you, or at a well, near a standing stone or in a place of beauty.

Say a pagan grace at important meals. The priestess Shan suggests simply: 'Thank you for giving your lives to feed ours.'

Take the time to contact trees, lean on them, sit by them and absorb them. If you sit quietly and calmly you will feel the essence of the tree, you may see pictures with your mind's eye or have a sense of 'knowing'. Keep a note of whatever you sense, for it will be very special.

Enjoy the earth, walk on her, breathe the air, touch the trees, and let your instincts tell you the way to live in harmony with her.

Further information

Elkington, John, and Hales, Julia, *The Green Consumer Guide*, Gollancz, 1988

Lovelock, J. E., *Gaia*, Oxford, 1987

The Green Circle – a fellowship of people interested in any of the following: magic, witchcraft, alternative healing, conservation, self-awareness or personal growth. SAE to PO Box 280, Maidstone ME16 0UL, England.

Greenpeace UK Office, Canonbury Villas, London N1 2PN, England. Tel. 0171 354 5100

Dragon National Network (Eco-magick, practical conservation and campaigning) SAE to Dragon, 3 Sanford Walk, New Cross, London, SE14 6NB, England. Tel. 0181 691 7685

Friends of the Earth, 26–28 Underwood St, London N1 7JQ, England. Tel. 0171 490 1555

Soil Association, 86 Colston St, Bristol BS1 5BB, England. Tel. 0117 929 0661. Promoting organic farming and protecting the environment – lists and information provided, for which there may be a small charge

Treespirit Reg. Charity, Hawkbatch Fm, Arley, Nr Bewdley, Worcs. DY12 3AH

Women's Environmental Network, 287 City Rd, London, EC1V 1LA. Tel. 0171 490 2511

Pagans on the Internet

Covenant of the Goddess USA World Wide Web
http://www.crc.ricoh.com/-rowanf/COG/iabout.html

House of the Goddess
I/N. hog@goddess.demon.co.uk
w/w/w. (shared with Dragon Environmental Group)
demon.co.uk/goddess.hog

Pagan Fed. http://www.tardis.ed.ac.uk/-ipf/pf.htw

appenδix

The fellowship of Isis

> *Growing numbers of people are discovering their love for the Goddess. At first this love may seem to be no more than an inner feeling. But soon it develops; it becomes a longing to help the Goddess actively in the manifestation of Her divine plan. Thus one hears such enquiries as, 'How can I get initiated into the Mysteries of the Goddess? How can I experience a closer communication with Her? Where are Her nearest temples and devotees? How can I join the priesthood of the Goddess?'*
>
> The Fellowship of Isis Manifesto

Membership of the Fellowship provides a means of closer communion with the Goddess Isis. This can be done singly, or by means of a larger group, called an 'Iseum'. The Fellowship was founded in 1976 by Lawrence, Pamela and Olivia Durdin-Robertson. There are now hundreds of Iseums and thousands of members. 'Love, Beauty and Truth are expressed through a multi-religious, multi-cultural, multi-racial Fellowship. The good in all faiths is honoured. Membership is free.'

The Fellowship is democratic and all members have equal privileges. Freedom of conscience is respected and no vows or commitments to secrecy are required. Activities are optional. Members are free to resign or join at their own choice. All Life is revered and the God is also venerated. Rites do not include sacrifice, actual or symbolic. Nature is revered and conserved and all religions tolerated.

Membership is open to all of every religion, tradition and race. Children are welcome subject to parental consent. The Fellowship believes in the promotion of Love, Beauty and Abundance. Friendliness, psychic gifts, happiness and compassion for all are encouraged, asceticism is not.

The college of Isis was suppressed 1,500 years ago but it has always been alive on the Inner Planes, and from these its return is inspired. Magi degrees may be conferred and correspondence courses are offered.

> *The Fellowship of Isis Priesthood is derived from an hereditary line of the Robertson from Ancient Egypt. Priestesses, Priests, every member have equal honour ... (and) work with the Goddess – or Goddess and God – of their own Faith. Every human, animal, bird, tree is an eternal offspring of the Mother Goddess's Divine Family of Life.*

For further information write to: The Fellowship of Isis, Clonegal Castle, Enniscorthy, Eire. Please enclose a self-addressed envelope and International Reply Coupons for a reply.

The Fellowship of Isis Handbook and *The College of the Isis Manual* are respectively £2, or US $4 Surface, US $5 Airmail, and £3, or US $6 Surface, US $7 by air. They are both by Olivia Robertson. The *Handbook* tells about the origin of the Fellowship, the nature of the Iseums, how to choose one and apply for ordination. The *Manual* describes how to choose a Lyceum, initiation and the Magi degree course. Information and prices are correct at Samhain 1995.

The Fellowship of Isis does much teaching through its lyceums all over the world, and it has done a great deal to put forward the message of the Great Goddess. It seems a welcoming organisation.

FURTHER
RESOURCES

The Pagan Federation have asked me to include some advice on joining groups, because very occasionally unscrupulous people do exploit the inexperienced. So be certain that you feel quite comfortable about anything you are asked to do. No genuine person would ever expect you to act in a way other than how you felt was right, so don't be taken in by someone who purports to know better than you what is correct for you. Unfortunately in any walk of life one meets the occasional person who is on a power trip, or who seeks to exploit sexually the unwary. The truly wise will never coerce, cajole, seduce or command. If you are on a pagan path you will value your freedom to choose and seek the Mysteries for yourself, so always retain that and your common sense.

If you wish to join a group the Federation can supply lists of those known to be ethical. Also if you have any questions about specific groups write to the Federation to see if they know anything about them. Remember to include a SAE. Not all contacts listed are known to me. Approach anything new with a sensible caution as you would in any other sphere of life.

NB: When writing to anyone or any organisation listed below or on preceding pages always include SAE or International Reply Coupons. Many pagan organisations operate on a shoestring.

Pagan Federation BM Box 7097, London WC1N 3XX, England. e-mail: Secretary @paganfed.demon.co.uk. The Pagan Federation also publish *Pagan Dawn* Magazine

House of the Goddess, 33 Oldridge Rd, London SW12 8PN, England. Tel. 0181 673 6370.
e-mail: I/N HOG@GODDESS.DEMON.CO.UK
W/W/W.DEMON.CO.UK/GODDESS.HOG (shared with Dragon Environmental Group)

Information service via leaflets on various pagan topics; send SAE and a short note on your particular interests. Publisher of *The Pagan Index* listing UK contacts, resources, groups. who's who, where's where. £5.99 in bookshops or post free direct from HOG. National Pagan Hallowe'en festival (Weekend after Hallowe'en)

Wood & Water Magazine, Goddess and feminist inclined, 77 Parliament Hill, London NW3 2TH England.

Talking Stick Magazine – myth, magic, paganism. PO Box 3719, London SW17 8XT

Pan Pacific Pagan Alliance, PO Box 719, Castlemaine. 3450, Australia

Church of All Worlds, PO Box 408, Woden ACT 2606, Australia, e-mail ftswk@cc.newcastle.edu.au

Circle Network News Magazine, PO Box 219, Mt Horeb. WI 53572 USA

Green Egg Magazine, Box 1542, Ukiah, CA 95482, USA

Wiccan Candle Magazine, 109 Vaughan Rd, Toronto, Ontario M6C 2L9 Canada

Grail Directory, Comprehensive directory of pagan resources, magazines etc. Worldwide, not just Australia. G.R.A.I.L Publications, GPO Box 1444, Canberra City 2601 ACT. Australia

Seventh Wave Music, PO Box 1, Totnes, Devon, TQ9 6UQ, UK – compelling music inspired by ancient pagan roots, lyrics sometimes quoted at chapter headings. Catalogue available.

Please contact the author via the publishers or by e-mail 100424.1723@compuserve.com

Other titles in this series

Chakras How to work with chakras, the body's energy centres, in safety and with confidence.

Chinese Horoscopes How to determine your own Chinese horoscope, what personality traits you are likely to have, and how your fortunes may fluctuate in years to come.

Dowsing How to start dowsing – what to use, what to dowse, and what to expect when subtle energies are detected.

Dream Interpretation How to unravel the meaning behind dream images to interpret your own and other people's dreams.

Feng Shui How to increase your good fortune and well-being by harmonising your environment with the natural energies of the earth.

Gems and Crystals All you need to know about choosing, keeping and using stones to increase your personal awareness and improve your well-being.

Graphology How to make a comprehensive analysis of your own and other people's handwriting to reveal the hidden self.

I Ching An introduction to the ancient beauty of the I Ching or Book of Changes – its history, survival and modern day applications.

Love Signs The important roles played by each of the planets, focusing particularly on the position of the Moon at the time of birth.

Meditation How to start meditating and benefiting from this ancient mental discipline immediately. Highly illustrated and full colour.

Numerology All the information you will need to understand the significance of numbers in your everyday life.

Palmistry What to look for and how to interpret what you find, using the oldest form of character reading still in use.

Runes How runes can be used in our technological age to increase personal awareness and stimulate individual growth.

Star Signs How your star sign affects everything about you. How to use this knowledge in your relationships and in everyday life.

Tarot Which cards to buy, where to get them and how to use them as a tool for gaining self-knowledge, while exploring present and future possibility. Full colour.

The Moon and You Analysis of the nine Lunar Types. How to find your moon phase and how to tune into it.

Visualisation How to practise the basic techniques – to relieve stress, improve your health and increase your sense of personal well-being.

Witchcraft An introduction to witchcraft dispelling the myths surrounding this ancient form of worship. How to celebrate the Sabbats and practise magic.

To order this series

All books in this series are available in bookshops or, in case of difficulty, can be ordered direct from the publisher. Just fill in the form below. Prices and availability subject to change without notice.

To : Hodder & Stoughton Ltd, Cash Sales Department, Bookpoint, 73c Milton Park, Abingdon, OXON, OX14 4TD, UK. If you have a credit card you may order by telephone – 01235 831700.

Please enclose a cheque or postal order made payable to Bookpoint Ltd, allowing the following for postage and packing: UK & BFPO: £1.00 for the first book, 50p for the second book and 30p for each additional book ordered up to a maximum charge of £3.00. OVERSEAS & EIRE: £2.00 for the first book, £1.00 for the second book and 50p for each additional book.

Please send me

	copies of 0 340 62082 X	Chakras	£4.99	£
	copies of 0 340 64804 X	Chinese Horoscopes	£5.99	£
	copies of 0 340 60882 X	Dowsing	£4.99	£
	copies of 0 340 60150 7	Dream Interpretation	£4.99	£
	copies of 0 340 62079 X	Feng-Shui	£4.99	£
	copies of 0 340 60883 8	Gems & Crystals	£5.99	£
	copies of 0 340 60625 8	Graphology	£4.99	£
	copies of 0 340 62080 3	I-Ching	£5.99	£
	copies of 0 340 64805 8	Love Signs	£4.99	£
	copies of 0 340 64835 X	Meditation	£5.99	£
	copies of 0 340 59551 5	Numerology	£4.99	£
	copies of 0 340 59552 3	Palmistry	£4.99	£
	copies of 0 340 62081 1	Runes	£4.99	£
	copies of 0 340 59553 1	Star Signs	£4.99	£
	copies of 0 340 59550 7	Tarot	£5.99	£
	copies of 0 340 64836 8	The Moon and You	£5.99	£
	copies of 0 340 65495 3	Visualisation	£5.99	£
	copies of 0 340 67014 2	Witchcraft	£5.99	£
			TOTAL	£

Name ....

Address ....

.... Post Code..................................

If you would prefer to pay by credit card, please complete:

Please debit my Visa/Access/Diner's Card/American Express (delete as appropriate) card no:

☐☐☐☐☐☐☐☐☐☐☐☐☐☐

Signature .... Expiry Date...

For sales in the following countries please contact:
UNITED STATES: Trafalgar Square (Vermont), Tel: 800 423 4525 (toll free)
CANADA: General Publishing (Ontario), Tel: 445 3333
AUSTRALIA: Hodder & Stoughton (Sydney), Tel: 02 638 5299